Mentoring

from the

Mountaintop

Rick Clendenen

Order additional copies of this book,
or contact Rick Clendenen via:
World Missions and Evangelism, Inc.
P. O. Box 790
Benton, KY 42025
Office: (270) 527-8369, Ext. 131

DEDICATION

Throughout our lives, we are given the opportunity to meet and influence thousands of people. In fact, I am told that regardless of whether we are an extrovert or introvert, the number of people we influence is around ten thousand. But how we influence them is the real essence of leadership. We can only do our best and pray that our influence positively influences others rather than negatively.

As I evaluate the relationships of my own life, I can truly say that other than Jesus Christ, no one has had such a positive influence in my life toward wholeness than has Dr. Evelyn Frye. Her compassion, support, and willingness to boldly confront my dysfunctions enabled me to grow and recover from destructive behavior patterns that were sure to shorten my life span. I now have a new lease on life.

Thanks to Dr. Frye, her assistant, Kathy, my loving wife, Debbie, our wonderful children, Renee and Landon, Richie and Jenny, and our grandson, Trey, I now have the support team in place to live a happy, healthy, and whole life. To them I dedicate this book, along with my life, to share the message of wholeness with the world. I Thessalonians 5:23 says it best: "And the very God of peace sanctify you wholly and I pray God your whole spirit and soul and body be preserved blameless until the coming of our Lord Jesus Christ."

ACKNOWLEDGEMENTS

It is rightly said that if you see a turtle perched on top of a fence post, be assured that he did not get there by himself. Concerning this book, I am that turtle. What you hold in your hand today is the combined effort of a number of people. In fact, I have had the privilege of working with three teams to whom I will forever be grateful.

I want to thank those who served as a part of the financial team for this book. Because of them, this dream has become a reality. With sincere appreciation I say thank you to Deena Philage, B.J. and Elsa Brown, Larry and Donna Smith, Dr. Bruce and Dee Wilson, and James and Debbie Rison. Their investment in me has resulted in me being able to invest in others.

The second team I want to acknowledge is the working team. I will never be able to repay my content editor and project manager, Marjorie Russell, my grammatical editor, Carolyn Buchholz, my dear friend and fellow author, José Bonilla, my photographer, John McCarroll, Jr, graphic designers Erica Weise and Marty Turner, and of course my wife Debbie, who spent countless hours typing and retyping this manuscript to generate the rough draft from which the others have worked. I say thank you from the bottom of my heart.

Last, but not least, is my support team made up of my spiritual fathers, as well as my spiritual sons, who worked with me to process the material contained within this book. The part they play in my life and in this book has been invaluable. And there's also my family who allowed me the time and the permission to share my story with the world.

Truly this has been a team effort and from one very grateful turtle, I say thanks.

MENTORING FROM THE MOUNTAINTOP

TABLE OF CONTENTS

INTRODUCTION

Nothing compares to the mountains. Not only are mountains places of tranquility and peace, but they offer a different perspective on the world. From the mountain, one can clearly see those things that are sometimes shrouded in the valley.

I was raised in the mountains. As my playground, the mountains offered unlimited possibilities—building clubhouses, hiking, swinging from grapevines, riding sleds in the winter snow. The mountains were forever before us, towering thousands of feet around our home. They spoke to me of a greatness beyond myself.

The mountains offered adventure. They held many species of animals, caves, cliffs, and varied terrain. But none of these could be experienced unless one was willing to make the climb. Climbing a mountain is difficult and cannot be accomplished without effort. Anyone who has climbed a mountain knows they're likely to fall a time or two, get dirty, skinned up, and exhausted. But oh, what joy to crest the mountain, breath in the deep air, and feel the accomplishment of hours of toiling and climbing. Reaching the top is worth the effort of overcoming the challenges of getting there.

As a child, I was often drawn to experience the serenity of the mountains. As I climbed upward, I left behind the noise of everyday living and seemed to enter the very presence of God, into a reverent silence. The peace was only occasionally interrupted by the call of a bird or by wind rustling through leaves. The mountains seemed to hold the secrets of life below.

God used mountains as settings from which to speak to His choice servants. Abraham was called to a mountain to sacrifice Isaac so God might judge his faithfulness. Moses was called to the mountain where God gave him the law. Elijah was called to a mountain where God revealed His power to His prophet. Throughout scripture, mountains were meeting places between God and man. Jesus used the mountains as a getaway for His disciples, a place where they could rest and receive instruction for the journey ahead.

As the pages of this book unfold, I will expound on the concept of mountain meetings with God. Since I was raised in the mountains, I appreciate their physical beauty. But as I walk through life, I realize that life itself is a series of mountains and valleys, a cycle of ascending and descending, ups and downs, challenges and victories.

Today I extend an invitation for you to climb above your circumstances, above the everyday hustle and bustle of life to where you can hear Him whispering your name. In the pages that follow, my desire is to share with you how God used intimate moments with Him – mountain moments – to bring wholeness to my life, healing me of the wounds I suffered in the valley experiences of my life. Raised in a dysfunctional home with more problems than answers, my life was filled with pain and emptiness. I discovered my need to follow Jesus, for only He had the answers to my dilemma.

As never before, God is calling to leaders, to those who will follow the example of Jesus in mentoring other leaders to carry on the work of His kingdom. But like the disciples of Jesus, like me, and even like Jesus Himself, you likely carry with you the pain of the valley. That's why I'm combining my story of healing with this teaching on mentoring. God heals us as we climb.

God desires not only to heal us, but also to make us whole. His love for us is greater than our pain. Now is the time to lace up your boots, gather your gear, and follow Jesus to the mountaintop. Happy climbing!

PROLOGUE

My breath is short ragged gasps as I climb. I question: Is this the trail I started on? Is this a trail at all? Zigzagging from ridge to ridge and then back again, this journey is more difficult than I first imagined. As I take another step, suddenly the unfamiliar ground seems to shift and I lose my footing. Gravity and my own momentum send me crashing into a cold wet pile of leaf litter and sod. Is anything more frightening than having what you thought was solid ground to suddenly collapse beneath you? As my heart races within me, I look around to see who witnessed my humiliation. With no progress lost, I can now relax for a moment.

While dampness from the ground soaks into my pants, I survey my situation. My goal is the top of the mountain. Funny how easy it was to see the top before I started climbing. But, looking back I can see that I have come a long way. Below me I can see houses and moving cars—all small from my vantage point. Those below me are completely unaware of my struggle. I could just turn around and go back, letting gravity have its way with me; for a time I consider that option. But there is just something about completing a job, finishing the course, something inside that makes me want to keep on going. So I labor to my feet and take a few more steps toward the prize. Maybe I should have prepared a bit more effectively for this hike. What started out as a pleasant afternoon stroll has turned into a challenge of endurance.

Nothing compares to a long hike in the mountains. Breezes blow through your hair, the air becomes more crisp and cool as you climb. But sometimes the way is treacherous and the footing unsure. There are ridges and valleys that must be scaled and descended. There are slippery slopes that can cause you to lose your balance and fall. Jagged rocks can cut deep and leave permanent scars. There are triumphs and tragedies along the way. But for both expert climber and novice hiker alike, nothing can replace the value of a reliable guide, a good mentor—someone who has already made the climb.

CHAPTER 1 | A PLACE OF SOLITUDE

AND HE GOETH UP INTO A MOUNTAIN, AND CALLETH UNTO HIM WHO HE WOULD: AND THEY CAME UNTO HIM. AND HE ORDAINED TWELVE, THAT THEY SHOULD BE WITH HIM, AND THAT HE MIGHT SEND THEM FORTH TO PREACH. (MARK 3:12-14)

My Christian journey began in 1963 when I was nine years old, at a time when my family lived in a six-room house in the picturesque mountains of eastern Kentucky. We lived at the base of Black Mountain, the highest point in the state, where the Appalachian and Blue Ridge Mountain ranges collide.

Life was simple in our little valley. The pace was slow, but the sense of community and family was strong. All the children played together. All the men worked together in the coal mines, and the men and boys even bathed together in a bath house belonging to United States Steel. In fact, we lived in a company town where everything—our homes and even the stores we shopped in—was owned by U.S. Steel.

Houses stood side by side with hardly any yard between them. Typical of many small communities, but especially true in ours, everyone knew everyone else's business. Because times were hard, we were forced to pull together to survive. Outwardly the residents of our community lived lives without boundaries, and because of that, privacy became a precious commodity. The emotional challenges of life were dealt with in private. We were taught to be strong, and not to complain. The prevailing philosophy was that life was not, nor would it ever be, easy, and only the strong would survive.

I was born December 1, 1954, the fourteenth child of Bill and Elsie Clendenen. Although ours was a Christian home, it certainly was not free of problems. Mixed into the normal stresses related to raising eleven surviving children was unresolved grief over a miscarriage, a stillborn birth, and the untimely death of my sister. At only ten months old, Sondra Gail died in my father's arms, an event that would forever change my father's life and, in turn, mine as well.

Sondra Gail's death was due to complications of an enlarged heart. Three months after her death, my sister Becky was born. When she was placed in my father's arms, instantly he transferred all of his love for, and grief over, Sondra Gail onto Becky. She became his baby girl and his healer.

Mother's next pregnancy was filled with complications and ended with a stillborn daughter. Devastated, she turned to Dad for comfort and help, but he was emotionally unavailable. The death of this daughter only reinforced his need for Becky. His emotional distance left Mother feeling abandoned, with an empty place in her heart and no support for her healing.

Soon she became pregnant again, this time with me—number fourteen in a twenty-year period. After my birth, Mom finally had someone to whom she could turn for healing. I became known as "Mama's little baby," a title I carried with pride. The unhealthy seeds of dysfunction were in place. Tensions grew between us children as jealousy caused us to fight one against another for the attentions of Mom and Dad.

Adding to the mix was our mentally retarded sister, Alice. The doctor had dropped her at birth, and the resulting brain damage caused scarring to her brain. This resulted in violent epileptic seizures occurring numerous times each day; in fact, I remember one day in particular when Alice suffered thirty-six seizures in a twenty-four hour period. In those days, little was known about how to help those who suffered as Alice did. Therefore, we were left to do the best we could in our attempt to have a normal life. With each seizure, Alice grew worse, her brain more scarred, her behavior more erratic and violent, and our home more troubled.

In 1963, the inevitable happened. With Mom and Dad away in town buying groceries and the other children outside playing, my sister Brenda found herself at home alone with Alice. The night before had been filled with seizures for Alice and she seemed dazed. She picked up a butcher knife and started toward Brenda, telling her she was going to kill her. Brenda tried to reason with Alice, tried to convince her to lay down the knife, but to no avail. In desperation, Brenda ran into the bathroom, managing to lock the door behind her. Alice stabbed the butcher knife through the door all the way to its handle over twenty times as Brenda stood on the other side, weeping and begging her to stop. Then as quickly as the incident began, it was over. Alice stopped, laid down the knife, and went into the living room.

A few moments later, Mom and Dad arrived home. They found Alice crying, and she told them that Brenda was locked in the bathroom and refused to play with her. After hearing our parents' voices, Brenda cautiously opened the door. Still visibly shaken, she told them the real story.

Mom and Dad realized it was no longer safe for Alice to live at home, but they didn't know what to do. Remember, this was 1963 and things were different then. After a lengthy search, a family friend referred them to the Kentucky Mental Institution in Danville, Kentucky, and my parents began negotiations to admit Alice there.

It was as if Alice seemed to sense what was coming. She grew extremely violent and out of control. There was nothing we could do to restrain her. Finally, to contain her, we were forced to lock her in two rooms of our house where she broke everything she could get her hands on and where she screamed night and day until she finally lost her voice.

After three days, this traumatic event seemed to come to an end as two men dressed in white came to our home in an ambulance. They sedated Alice like a wild animal, strapped her to a gurney and carried her away. As I stood on the porch, watching them load Alice into the ambulance, she looked up at me. Our eyes made contact, and I could sense her crying out for help. But what could I do? I was just a little boy of nine and the problem was far beyond my ability to change. I was overwhelmed with helplessness and would forever remember that moment when I turned away and went back into the house, wiping away my tears and closing the door behind me.

Inside, everything had instantly turned from mass hysteria and chaos to an eerie silence. Outwardly it seemed the problem was behind us, but we were left alone to deal with our private pain behind closed doors. Never would my family sit down together and discuss our feelings of loss nor would we be allowed to talk about it with anyone else outside the family.

This horrible experience so devastated us that everyone was emotionally drained. It affected Mom in a much different way, though. She snapped under the pressure and began to scream. Doctors confirmed a nervous breakdown. For weeks, I was awakened by her screams as she tried to cope with the loss of Alice.

As often happens in the midst of trying times, God began to reveal Himself to me. As Mom recovered enough to attend church, we once again began making our way across the mountain to the independent Pentecostal church in Appalachia, Virginia. In fact, we went to church every time the doors were opened, no questions asked. I believe Mom and Dad sensed that our only chance for survival was God.

One particular night the church service began as normally as most others I had witnessed my entire life, but then suddenly became very different. Even as a young boy, I could sense something unusual taking place. A holy hush swept across the church as the presence of God filled the place. People began to weep and pray aloud. I saw Mom and Dad make their way to the altar. As they were praying, I saw my opportunity to slip away from the pew. (That was a real no-no! Mom sat at one end of the pew, Dad at the other, and we children sat between them without making a peep.) But that night I found myself sitting on the platform with my legs between the banister rails, looking out toward the congregation. No one seemed to notice that I was there because of the presence of God.

What I saw next defies explanation, for it looked as if a cloud filled that country church. A crippled man I had known all my life suddenly jumped to his feet, his wheelchair turning over behind him. It was a true miracle—he could walk! My sister, Brenda, who had a goiter the size of my fist, was instantly healed before my eyes. I had never seen anything like it before. After a few minutes, everything seemed to return to normal, but I never would.

I remember the next day vividly. There I was, a nine-year-old boy lying on my special place, the cellar door at the side of our house. It was my thinking spot where I often laid for hours looking at the sky, imagining what God was really like. That day there was a lot to think about. Kenneth could walk, Brenda was healed, Mom was better, and suddenly I realized that God was real! He was more now than just a thought or a feeling. "God," I remember saying out loud, "You're for real and that ain't no joke! I saw You last night."

The realness of God saturated me at that moment, and I felt that God was calling me to a lifelong journey. I wanted to discover as much as I could possibly know about God. Maybe He could answer the questions that had haunted me my entire life: Why was Alice like she was? Why was Dad so angry? Why was Mom so afraid? Why did I feel so alone in a house full of people? Surely this living Jesus, looking down on a little boy, could answer a few simple questions and make me whole. But the answers didn't come as quickly as I thought they would. In fact, as time passed I watched the members of my family continue to deal with their pain in their own way.

In life, every individual deals with trauma. Trauma, in turn, causes pain. And anger is the emotional response to pain. How we process anger will determine the quality of our life. In my life, I turned to food, and in particular, to sweets. I discovered that sugar soothed my emotions and temporarily helped me handle my negative feelings. I didn't know where else to turn.

After mother's breakdown, Alice was never mentioned again. It was if she had never existed. I know that sounds strange, but it isn't, really. In most cases, when real trauma occurs, our minds kick into overload. We seek to block out the events as best we can, and we only deal with what we must to survive. We build defense mechanisms that keep the world at bay, while forgetting that these same fences keep us imprisoned.

Years went by before I realized how the chain of events in my family's life had crippled me emotionally. If you had asked me back then to describe our family, I would have considered our life normal, whatever that is. We were just playing the hand that life had dealt us, trying to get along. But, thank God, Jesus never came to just help us get along, but rather to make us whole so we might be overcomers. He extends to us an invitation in Matthew 11:28–29: "Come unto Me, all ye that labor and are heavy laden, and I will give you rest. Take My yoke upon you, and learn of Me; for I am meek and lowly in heart: and ye shall find rest unto your souls."

Jesus offered a similar invitation to twelve dysfunctional men who were living out mundane lives in various occupations with no hope of success or wholeness. That invitation is found in Mark 3:13–15: "And He goeth up into a mountain, and calleth unto Him whom He would: and they came unto Him. And He ordained twelve, that they should be with Him, and that He might send them forth to preach, And to have power to heal sicknesses, and to cast out devils…"

Jesus took His disciples to a mountain, away from the crowd, away from everyday life and the opinions of others, to a place where they would have no need to fit in to the expectations of any other person. The mountain was a place of solitude where they might be able to gain His perspective for dealing with life and where they might find rest and healing for their souls. He was offering them not only a way to wholeness, but a brand new beginning and a future filled with hope. He was willing to mentor them through their pain so they might reach their potential.

How would this mentoring transpire? It would hinge on three simple statements made by Jesus: "Follow Me," "Come unto Me... and learn of Me," and "Go in My name (paraphrased)." Let's examine the power of these three statements in the process of discipleship.

Follow Me

As recorded in Matthew 4:19, Jesus invited a couple of professional fishermen to "Follow Me." He gave the same invitational command to all of His disciples, a group that included Simon (whom Jesus renamed Peter), James and John (nicknamed The Sons of Thunder by Jesus), Andrew, Phillip, Bartholomew, Matthew, Thomas, James, Thaddaeus, Simon, and Judas—a group of no-name social misfits and religious outcasts. These men certainly were not the cream of the crop. Jesus passed by those who deemed themselves valuable and offered Himself to those who realized they were nothing.

What was His offer? It was Himself, His friendship, His continual companionship. His first instruction was "Follow Me!" In telling them to "Follow Me" Jesus was testing their faithfulness. Jesus never expected them to have all the answers. In fact, He knew they were inadequate for the job at hand. "Follow Me" was a simple command. All He was saying was, "I want you to witness what I do. I have no expectations for you but to show up." As we follow Him, we learn by example how to deal with things as He would deal with them, to speak what He would speak, to act as He would act. "Just follow Me," Jesus said, and in doing so, He examined their faithfulness. This led Him to His second command.

"Come Unto Me... and Learn of Me"

Only Jesus understood the gravity of His invitation recorded in Matthew 11:28–29 when He implored His disciples, "Come unto Me and learn of Me." Since ministry is nothing more than an overflow of our personal relationship with Jesus Christ, Jesus was calling them to a deeper level of commitment in their relationship with Him.

Literally thousands of people were following Him, but with their own agendas. Would the disciples be different? Would they be willing to enter into a more intimate relationship? In the English language, the word intimacy, spoken slowly, sounds very much like the words "into me see," and this is a wonderful definition of the term. To truly be intimate with each other, individuals must enter a relationship transparent, without hidden agendas or comfort of covering, offering themselves stripped, open, and honest to one another.

In this challenge Jesus was testing their vulnerability and teachability. Could they be trusted? Would they be loyal? Would they remain committed to the mentoring relationship Jesus was offering even when they were corrected? Often we cringe and walk away from such invitations, afraid to face the truth and deal with our egos, our pride, and our wrong motives.

To grow, we must be willing to learn. In order to learn we must admit that we don't know it all! Teachability is a true sign of maturity. None of us will ever know it all, but one thing is certain: we can save ourselves a lot of grief and misery by answering His call to mentorship.

"Go in My Name"

In this paraphrased statement from Mark 3:14, Jesus was testing his disciples' obedience. Now that they were faithful and able to receive instruction and correction, could they represent Him instead of their own agendas?

> *EVIDENCE OF MATURITY IS REVEALED IN THE ABILITY TO REPRESENT SOMEONE ELSE WITH LOYALTY AND FAITHFULNESS.*

Evidence of maturity is revealed in the ability to represent someone else with loyalty and faithfulness. Jesus put it this way in Luke 16:12: "And if ye have not been faithful in that which is another man's, who shall give you that which is your own?" Faithfulness and loyalty are exemplified in how we represent those in authority.

In the lives of the disciples, one of their struggles revolved around their own agendas and egos. Although they followed Jesus, they argued among themselves about which one was the greatest, even as the greatest One was humbly serving their needs. The same is true in ministry. If we are unwilling to lay down our agenda, pick up our cross, and follow Him, our ego can hinder us from having a significant ministry with eternal impact.

When Jesus invited those who would be identified as His disciples to follow Him and be faithful, to go with Him and learn and be teachable, and to be obedient and loyal, He was offering things we can only learn in solitude and intimacy with the Lord Jesus Christ. These are not the fruits of public ministry but of private intimacy as we follow Him to the mountain and learn to become servant leaders. But how does that happen? The answer is by responding to the call.

THE CALL

> "YE HAVE NOT CHOSEN ME, BUT I HAVE CHOSEN YOU, AND ORDAINED YOU, THAT YE SHOULD GO AND BRING FORTH FRUIT, AND THAT YOUR FRUIT SHOULD REMAIN: THAT WHATSOEVER YE SHALL ASK OF THE FATHER IN MY NAME, HE MAY GIVE IT YOU." (JOHN 15:16)

This verse of scripture reveals three important principles that we must understand in order to carry out our roles as servant leaders: Proclamation, purpose, and promise.

Proclamation

"Ye have not chosen Me, but I have chosen you..." (John 15:16) What wonderful news! You have been chosen by God. You did not seek Him, but He has sought you and extended His hands of love towards you. He desires you to be a part of His family, His church, and His bride. Nothing should bring you more comfort or confidence than the realization of His desire to include you in His glorious Kingdom.

Suddenly my mind goes back to my school days when everything seemed to center around sports and games. I recall the horrid feelings of standing with a group of boys waiting to be chosen on a team. How dehumanizing! Since I was overweight as a child, I always encouraged the fellows to play football where my chances of being chosen first were much greater. Nothing was more humiliating than to be chosen last: it was as if I hadn't been chosen at all, but that those choosing merely had no other options.

This is not so with God. The Creator of the universe, with every option available to Him, has chosen you to play on His team. This choice was not based on your talents, your abilities, or your capacity to contribute, but rather on His loving nature and His desire to have a relationship with you.

Purpose

"...that you might bear fruit and that your fruit should remain..." (John 15:16) God's call always centers around His purpose, and His purpose involves the redemption of man. We cannot answer the call of God without embracing His purpose. The word "ordained" means to be set apart with purpose.

Many believers in the body of Christ only view themselves as being called out from the world. The word "church" comes from the Greek word, ecclesia, meaning "the called-out ones." Most Christians, though, never seem to concern themselves with what they have been called to. Jesus simply states His two-fold purpose for what we are called to: "that you might bear fruit and that your fruit should remain..." His first desire is for your personal fruitfulness, that you might experience the fullness of His grace and allow Him to make you whole. This process of wholeness includes every area of our lives: spiritual, mental, emotional, physical, and material.

The Bible declares: "Beloved, I wish above all things that thou mayest prosper and be in health, even as thy soul prospereth" (3 John:2). God's purpose includes your wholeness. Jeremiah 29:11 says: "For I know the thoughts that I think toward you, saith the Lord, thoughts of peace, and not of evil, to give you an expected end."

God's ultimate desire and purpose for your life is that you might be whole, abundantly fruitful, walking in victory, and exercising authority over the enemy. He has said that He wants this for us, and it is critical to our lives and our eternal impact that we believe Him.

Secondly, He states that your fruit should remain. We must remember that personal fruitfulness will always result in public fruitfulness. Jesus declared in Matthew 7:20: "Wherefore by their fruits ye shall know them." The word "remain" in John 15:16 speaks of continuation. The true purpose of fruitfulness is to produce seed for the next generation and for generations to follow. Jesus is the source of all life. Within everything He created is found the seed for multiplication and continuation. Our success as leaders cannot be judged by what we have accomplished in our lifetime, but rather, how we affect generations that follow and how we impact eternity. A life well spent is a life invested in generations to come.

Paul commends the process of continuation in the life of Timothy: "...when I call to remembrance the unfeigned faith that is in thee, which dwelt first in thy grandmother Lois, and thy mother Eunice; and I am persuaded that in thee also" (2 Timothy 1:5). This, my friend, is lasting fruitfulness. And this is the standard of true success. Future generations must know the purpose for which we gave our lives and must be committed to take the Gospel of Jesus Christ to the uttermost parts of the earth. Herein is the driving force for all evangelism, discipleship, and mentoring.

Promise

"...that whatsoever ye shall ask of the Father in my name, He may give it you" (John 15:16). What a promise! The Almighty God, creator of heaven and earth has, by His word, committed Himself to help you carry out His purpose in your life. Notice this is not just any purpose, but His purpose.

We have been given the promise that He will hear our cry and answer our prayer. But He has also given another promise—His promise of power to carry out the task. Acts 1:8 declares: "But ye shall receive power, after that the Holy Ghost is come upon you: and ye shall be witnesses unto Me both in Jerusalem, and in all Judea, and in Samaria, and unto the uttermost part of the earth."

Even better than His promise to hear and answer prayer, and even greater than His promise of power to accomplish the task, is the ultimate promise of His continual presence. Matthew 28:19–20 says: "Go ye therefore, and teach all nations, baptizing them in the name of the Father, and of the Son, and of the Holy Ghost: Teaching them to observe all things whatsoever I have commanded you: and, lo, I am with you alway, even unto the end of the world."

Regardless of what I face on the journey, one thing is certain—I won't have to face it alone for He is with me.

Jesus Himself is fulfilling His purpose through my life. I am only the vessel. He is the source of life. The key to successful leadership is His presence within the individual. Throughout the Bible, God never called people to do anything without extending His hand of partnership to them, and without also giving the promise that He would be their source and their constant companion. Therefore, God has promised all of us that if we will embrace His purpose, we can, without doubt, expect to experience His power and His presence.

Too often when we are consumed with our selfish dreams and our own vain ambitions we blame God either for not moving on our behalf or for not coming to our defense. We fail to understand that His promises, His power, and His presence can only accompany His purpose. God has not promised to bless our mess; therefore, we would be wise to allow God to set the agenda, teach us the vital lessons we need to learn and become actively involved in what He is doing. As we embrace His purpose, His blessing is automatic.

As we make our journey up the mountain, some serious questions must be asked. Are you willing to become real and transparent? Are you willing for Him to teach and correct you? Are you willing to exchange success for wholeness? Remember that only whole people can reproduce whole people. We teach what we know but we reproduce what we are! If your answers to these questions are yes, then you are ready to climb the mountain, to be taught the principles of servant leadership as only Jesus can teach them.

CHAPTER 2 | MOUNTAIN OF TEMPTATION

THEN WAS JESUS LED UP OF THE SPIRIT INTO THE WILDERNESS TO BE TEMPTED OF THE DEVIL. AGAIN, THE DEVIL TAKETH HIM UP INTO AN EXCEEDING HIGH MOUNTAIN, AND SHEWETH HIM ALL THE KINGDOMS OF THE WORLD, AND THE GLORY OF THEM... (MATTHEW 4:1, 8A)

What troubling words! Jesus, led by the Spirit into the wilderness. How could a loving Father lead His only Son into a wilderness? One thing is certain, He had a reason, an ultimate purpose. Nothing ever touches our lives without first being sifted through the fingers of God. Romans 8:28 is still true: "And we know that all things work together for good to them that love God, to them who are the called according to His purpose."

The Judean mountains are unlike any other. I've had the privilege of traveling around the world a number of times and have witnessed the beauty of the Balkan Mountains, the

> *NOTHING EVER TOUCHES OUR LIVES WITHOUT FIRST BEING SIFTED THROUGH THE FINGERS OF GOD.*

Carpathians, the Alps, the Rockies, the Andes, and others. But nothing prepared me for what I would experience as we left Jerusalem in a van headed toward Jordan. As we approached the Judean wilderness, my mind flashed to the Matthew 4 account of Jesus in the wilderness. I wondered how He could have even survived an ordeal like that in such a place.

The Judean wilderness is nothing more than a mountainous desert, stripped of foliage and trees. Nothing shades you from the scorching sun, and only an occasional rock prevents wind-driven sand from blasting against your face. It is quite literally the most barren place I have ever seen. And Jesus spent forty days there alone, fasting, without basic provisions, and with only God, His Father, to strengthen Him. And in this wilderness, the purpose of God was to strengthen Him for the temptation ahead.

A number of years ago, in what I can only define as a moment of temporary insanity, I agreed to lift weights with a retired Marine. What resulted was a painful, but memorable, experience. He had converted his garage into an ancient version of a gym. He was like a cave man when it came to lifting; there was no fancy equipment but rather buckets filled with concrete, hooked to pulley systems, a rigging that provided nearly every exercise known to man.

We started with bench presses. As he positioned himself on the bench, I nervously began to count the weights on the bar— 230 pounds! He began to snort and huff like a train leaving the station, and time after time, he lifted this enormous amount. As he strained to lift the weight, his stomach seemed to vanish into his chest with muscles bulging as if they were trying to escape his skin. It was a sight to behold.

Then came my turn. I swallowed hard as I took my place on the bench. I began to breathe and snort as I had seen him do, but when I grabbed the bar, nothing moved. My stomach muscles stayed right where they had always been and so did the weights. Embarrassed, I muttered, "Maybe we need to take off a little weight. What do you think?" So we removed some weight, and then more. This process continued several times until finally I was looking up at a total of only ninety pounds, bar and all. The ninety pound weakling—you guessed it!

As I began to lift, my arms throbbed in pain. I wanted so badly to run to my car and make a quick getaway, but I was too ashamed. Over and over I suggested that maybe I should start out slowly, but nothing would suit him but a full workout. I was using muscles I didn't even know I possessed.

Finally it was over. Dripping in sweat, totally exhausted, and smiling in an effort to hold back tears of pain, I made my way to my car and eased into the driver's seat. Mike looked in the window and made a strange statement. "You're stronger now," he said. Bewildered, and thinking I couldn't have heard correctly, I asked "What did you say?" and he repeated, "You're stronger now!"

Sarcastically I responded, "Would you like to expound on that statement?"

"Let me explain to you how this works," he said. "A muscle cannot build up stronger until it is broken down and depleted of all its present strength. And then it comes back stronger than ever."

Suddenly I heard the words of the Apostle Paul in 2 Corinthians 12:9 echoing from centuries past in my spirit: "My strength is made perfect in weakness." God allows trying times to come. He allows the weight of the world to be placed upon our shoulders, not to break us, but to build us and our character. I get it now! Trials and temptations will come, but God uses them to strengthen us.

Throughout history, the Bible revealed great leaders who emerged from the wilderness. Among them were Abraham,

Moses, David, Elijah, John the Baptist, and the greatest leader of all, the Lord Jesus Christ. They all had their wilderness time but the question remains: Why the wilderness?

God's three-fold purpose for the wilderness season is revealed in Deuteronomy 8:2: "And thou shalt remember all the way which the Lord thy God led thee these forty years in the wilderness; to humble thee, and to prove thee, to know what was in thine heart, whether thou wouldest keep His commands, or no."

To Humble Us

Humility is best when it is self-inflicted. In fact, the book of James encourages us to humble ourselves under the mighty hand of God. Unfortunately, most of the time we move too slowly for God, so He helps us by humbling us through trials, tribulations and temptations.

> *OUR LEVEL OF AUTHORITY WILL ALWAYS BE EQUAL TO OUR LEVEL OF SUBMISSION TO PROPER AUTHORITY.*

Humility is described as the act of becoming teachable and meek. Humility is the only prerequisite for learning. We must come to the awareness of our need and inadequacy. We also must learn the power of submitting to the proper authorities, allowing them to instruct, correct, and reprove us.

Leadership is a lifestyle, not a position. Our level of authority will always be equal to our level of submission to proper authority. There can be no true promotion without humility.

To Prove Us

As an inventor would test his product with pride, not to expose its weakness, but rather to prove its strength, so it is with

God. God's ultimate goal is to bring out the best in us. In the Bible there is no greater example of this than the life of Job. God allowed Satan to test Job because He knew Job could stand the test.

We find a comforting promise in 1 Corinthians 10:13: "There hath no temptation taken you but such as is common to man: but God is faithful, who will not suffer you to be tempted above that ye are able; but will with the temptation also make a way to escape, that ye may be able to bear it."

Be sure of this one thing: God knows our limitations.

To Know Our Hearts

Often our life is like a tomato—when pressure is applied, what is inside gushes out. Trials have a way of opening our hearts and revealing our true motives. God is more interested in the motives of our hearts than in the actions of our hands. The adversities each of us faces on a daily basis should strengthen our resolve to be a leader with character. It is in difficult times that we are able to determine whether our trust and dependency have truly been in God or in our own gifts and abilities. The question we must ask ourselves is: Do I really trust God? Be assured, my friend, He knows you better than you know yourself. He also knows the future, and the trial you face today is preparing you for the mountain you must climb tomorrow. So it was in the life of Jesus, our example. His time in the wilderness prepared Him for the cross.

The temptation of Jesus in the wilderness was timed to perfection. It came at the end of a forty-day fast, when Jesus was physically weak and alone. I've noticed the same thing in my life. Quite often the enemy attacks when I feel weak and exhausted.

The same was true in the life of Elijah. It was after his greatest success on Mount Carmel that he sat alone in the wilderness under a juniper tree, praying to die. Satan is cunning in his attack and relentless in his desire to destroy you and your influence.

PREPARATION FOR THE WILDERNESS

The last prophecy in the Old Testament is found in Malachi 4:5–6: "Behold I will send you Elijah the prophet before the great and dreadful day of the Lord. And He shall turn the hearts of the fathers to the children and the hearts of the children to the fathers less I come and smite the earth with a curse."

The curse of our world is fatherlessness. Our jails and prisons are full of people who lack the example of a father in their lives. Recently, I had the opportunity to visit two of the largest prisons in our nation. I spent two days with prisoners on death row. As we retraced the steps that led them to death row, all of them seemed to have one thing in common—a dysfunctional relationship with their father. Either their father was abusive or absent altogether. None of them seemed to have a strong father figure in their lives. Over and over we returned to the same curse—fatherlessness. We should realize that it is easier to build a man than it is to repair one.

The Hebrew culture was a gender-biased culture where females were viewed as property; their value was little different than that of livestock. Education was only offered to the male children. This educational system was known as pedagogues, a word actually meaning, "learning to walk according to the law of God." Paul makes reference to this system and its symbolic significance to us as children of God in chapters 3 and 4 of the book of Galatians. However, as Paul speaks of our development and maturity as Christians, he makes clear that there is no distinction between male or female, bond or free, Jew or gentile in the Kingdom of God. In 1 John 3:1–2, the Bible says that we are all the sons of God. So God has no daughters, no grandchildren, no stepchildren—we are all sons. Therefore, He treats us as sons. The word son is a unique term given to a child who had experienced pedagogues. Let me explain to you the pedagogues system.

Age 0–3: The child is taught by his mother until he is weaned.

Age 3–5: The child is dressed as a servant, placed with them to be trained, and the servants begin to read to him from the written law (Torah).

Age 5: He is enrolled in Hebrew school and begins to memorize the Torah for himself.

Age 10: He memorizes the oral law (Mishna).

Age 12: Bar-Mitzvah: This ceremony is the time for adoption.

At Bar-Mitzvah, the young man is brought before his family to quote the oral and written law. In response, his father adopts him. The word "adoption" means, "the placing of a son in full rank." During the ceremony the father removes from him the clothes of a servant, places on him his own robe, puts a ring upon his finger and shoes on his feet. The robe represents the father's identity, the ring represents the father's authority, and the shoes represent the young man's destiny. From that moment, he is no longer referred to as a child, but as a son. He has full rights in decision-making processes. He can represent his father in business, and he possesses full rights to his inheritance. Contrasting that, today we can see the sad lack of fatherhood that results in a loss of identity, authority, and destiny in the lives of sons.

Notice the three areas in which the devil focused his attacks on Jesus. Satan's efforts centered on Jesus' identity, His authority, and His destiny.

His Identity

"If thou be the Son of God, cast Yourself down" (Matthew 4:6). Long before the birth of Jesus, Satan had birthed a myth that the real Messiah would come floating down from the pinnacle of the temple. Notice that Satan's opening statements of temptation were a reflection of that lie, but they began with a challenge to His relationship with His Father, casting doubt upon His role as a Son: "If thou be the Son of God..." Since many of us have not had a proper relationship with our earthly father, we struggle with a relationship with our Heavenly Father, opening the door for Satan's attack against our identity. If this is true in your case, the primary spirit you will have to contend with is the spirit of confusion. The spirit of confusion came against Jesus saying, in effect, "Which Messiah are you going to be, a floating, glorious Messiah or a suffering Messiah?"

His Authority

"All these things I will give thee, if thou wilt fall down and worship me" (Matthew 4:9). Satan was offering Jesus the kingdoms of the world in exchange for His worship. Be aware that Satan always offers power in exchange for authority. But authority is much greater than power. Authority is the right to rule; power is the force to rule. Authority can only come from those in authority and all legal authority is delegated.

The spirit at work in Satan's temptation of Jesus is easy to identify as the spirit of control (the Jezebel spirit). The spirit of confusion comes against your past, but the spirit of control comes against you in the present. Satan was offering Jesus a crown without a cross. But Jesus knew who His Father was and He also knew who He was.

His Destiny

"If thou be the Son of God, command that these stones be made bread" (Matthew 4:3). The third temptation of Jesus targeted the appetite of the flesh. Satan hoped that Jesus would lose sight of His long-range vision of the cross in order to meet His temporary need for food. With this temptation, Jesus faced the spirit of seduction that appeals to fleshly appetites. Satan will offer to buy your future for whatever appeals to you through the lust of the flesh, the lust of the eyes, or the pride of life. In comparison to what God has in store for you as His heir and joint heir with Jesus Christ, this temptation is at best nothing more than a piece of bread, one for which it is hardly worth trading your future.

Jesus displayed the victory of a servant leader against temptation. Like Him, we too can stand against the spirit of confusion, the spirit of control, and the spirit of seduction by using the same keys to victory that Jesus used: 1) knowing who our Father is; 2) knowing the authority He has given us through the Lord Jesus Christ; and 3) knowing clearly our mission and future.

Note what John 13:3–5 says of Jesus: "Jesus knowing that the Father had given all things into His hands, and that He was come from God, and went to God; He riseth from supper, and laid aside His garments; and took a towel, and girded Himself. After that He poureth water into a basin, and began to wash the disciples' feet, and to wipe them with the towel wherewith He was girded."

I thank God for the spiritual fathers He has brought into my life: Dr. J.T. Parish, Dr. David Parish, and Dr. Dale Yerton. Through their mentorship and love, I have learned my identity, my authority, and my destiny. And now I am able not only to stand against the "wiles of the devil" (Ephesians 6:11), but also to raise up spiritual sons, thus continuing the lineage that was imparted to me.

Paul addressed fatherhood issues in 1 Corinthian 4:15 when he stated: "For though ye have ten thousand instructors in Christ, yet have ye not many fathers..." Without earthly and spiritual fathers in our lives, we often find ourselves struggling to relate to God as Father. The church resembles an orphanage: the members look in anticipation to the next one coming through the door, hoping that person will be their father and bring an end to the struggles they face within. Now is the time for the church to arise, to take its proper place in providing mentors and spiritual fathers to equip the next generation to be sons of God and operate in their identity, authority, and destiny.

As I close this chapter, let me encourage you to begin praying that God will bring into your life those destined to mentor you into the fullness of your identity, authority, and destiny in Him. For only when these issues are settled will you be ready to climb higher up the mountain with Him.

CHAPTER 3 | MOUNTAIN OF INSTRUCTION

ONE DAY AS THE CROWDS WERE GATHERING, JESUS WENT UP THE
MOUNTAINSIDE WITH HIS DISCIPLES AND SAT DOWN TO TEACH THEM.
(MATTHEW 5:1; NLT)

The grass covered mountain near the Sea of Galilee was a cozy setting. Like all good teachers, Jesus knew that a pleasant environment sets an atmosphere for learning. Therefore, He had selected a perfect place to deal with a delicate subject— education. His disciples were unlearned men without formal religious training, commoners, if you will. But they were also under the assumption that they were on a fast track to Kingdom position. Why would they need instruction? After all, they knew the King Himself. As the old adage goes, it's not what you know but who you know, right?

Let me take a moment to dispel this myth. There is no such thing as a fast track to success and significance, and everyone who arrives there must walk step by step. The path each of us chooses may vary from that of others, but the requirements of knowledge and experience remain the same. All of us have the same starting place. We usually begin with a great ambition to succeed but are ignorant of the steps necessary to achieve success and are completely oblivious to the price we will pay along the journey.

> THERE IS NO SUCH THING AS A FAST TRACK TO SUCCESS AND SIGNIFICANCE, AND EVERYONE WHO ARRIVES THERE MUST WALK STEP BY STEP.

In Romans 10:2, Paul describes each Christian as he leaves the starting gate: "For I bear them record that they have a zeal of God but not according to knowledge." How would Jesus, the master teacher, approach the subject of the need for learning without destroying His disciples' natural enthusiasm? The struggle all mentors face is telling those who think they have arrived and believe they have all the answers that there are actually some things yet to learn.

Imagine how the disciples felt. After years of eking out a mundane living, suddenly they were handpicked to be leaders of a new, emerging kingdom. The religious leaders they had admired were passed by for such a promotion while the disciples, for some unknown reason, had been selected. On top of this, thousands of people were gathering around them, and they were feeling the fame of being associated with the new King. Could it get any better than this? All of it was a bit overwhelming for a group of hometown boys. The headlines might read: LOCAL BOYS MAKE BIG.

The air was filled with excitement that day on the mountainside. The disciples could sense something important was about to happen but they really didn't know what. Maybe Jesus would use this opportunity to announce their kingdom position before the waiting crowd. They gathered as close as possible around Jesus, but to their surprise, no announcement came. Instead, Jesus began teaching the lesson of the day.

"Blessed are the poor in spirit: for theirs is the Kingdom of Heaven. Blessed are they that mourn: for they shall be comforted. Blessed are the meek: for they shall inherit the earth. Blessed are they which do hunger and thirst after righteousness: for they shall be filled. Blessed are the merciful: for they shall obtain mercy.

Blessed are the pure in heart: for they shall see God. Blessed are the peacemakers: for they shall be called the children of God. Blessed are they which are persecuted for righteousness' sake: for theirs is the Kingdom of Heaven. Blessed are ye, when men shall revile you, and persecute you, and shall say all manner of evil against you falsely, for my sake. Rejoice, and be exceeding glad: for great is your reward in heaven: for so persecuted they the prophets which were before you" (Matthew 5:3–12).

Without pausing, Jesus continued on, dismantling the disciples' unsanctified ambitions by introducing them to teachings on humility, meekness, righteousness, persecution, and more. The disciples were shocked, perhaps thinking to themselves, "What are You talking about, Jesus, and what does this have to do with us and Your Kingdom?" Even with the passage of time one can almost feel tensions mounting as each realized they were unqualified for the job. But even more so, the innermost feelings of their lives were being challenged. Peter's pride had been assaulted; Matthew's struggle with rejection was trying to surface; insecure Thomas doubted whether or not he could do this, and wondered if it was more than he signed up for. Jesus, like a skilled marksman, continued, shifting His sermon from their attitudes to their influence, to their example, to their commitment, to their purity, to their loyalty, to their love, to their prayer life, to their giving, until finally, He closed the session by dealing with judgmentalism.

In a matter of a few minutes Jesus touched their problems personally, laying out for them not a lesson, but a format or lifestyle that they would have to embrace and incorporate in order to be a part of His Kingdom. We know this sermon text as the greatest sermon ever given, the Sermon on the Mount. But the disciples, as they sat at the feet of Jesus, were experiencing the greatest challenge of all time. How could they perform at the level Jesus had described, especially without any formal religious training or previous experience?

As I read this story, it brings up a haunting memory. The year was 1972 and I was graduating from high school with a cheated diploma. I had hated school, but I was more afraid of what life was offering me after that night. Physically abused by a junior high school teacher, I was turned off by the entire education system. Back then, my purpose for living was clear—to cause those in the educational system as much pain as they had caused me. I was constantly in trouble, spending more time in the principal's office than I did in the classroom. But finally, my graduation day arrived. This would be the end and, man, was I happy! As I sat in the dimly lit auditorium, name after name was called. Then at last came the moment I had longed for: "Richard Dale Clendenen" rang out over the PA system and I made my way to the stage. As I crossed the stage, the principal I had learned to hate extended his hand to congratulate me. What a joke!

While clutching my right hand, he placed the diploma in my left and leaned toward me to whisper the words, "This day could not possibly make you as happy as it does me." I took the diploma and laughed in his face, thinking to myself, "It's over now. Good riddance!"

As I walked away, feeling a sense of victory, I was completely unprepared for what awaited me. Within three months of that momentous occasion, my life had spiraled completely out of control and I found myself in Dallas, Texas, in more trouble than I could handle. Things were so bad that I stood looking into a mirror and contemplated suicide with a razor blade poised on my arm. What would I do now? There was no one to blame but myself. I had made some stupid choices. I had left home in rebellion against Mom and Dad and with a resolve that no longer was anyone going to tell me what to do. In fact, no one was going to rule my life but me. My life belonged to me and I was going to live it.

When I went to Dallas, I moved in with my sister, Nancy. Although the third oldest in our family, Nancy was number one when it came to rebellion. Since I was also in rebellion, we seemed like a perfect fit. But when I arrived at Nancy's home, it didn't take me long to discover that she had real problems. Addicted to drugs, she sponsored her habit by going from one "sugar daddy" relationship to another. I soon found myself tangled in a new web Nancy spun for me with the aid of one of her prostitute friends. Together they devised a plan to take advantage of my youthful ignorance and then to blackmail me. The trap was set, the bait was ready, and I walked right into it. Caught, and with no way out, man did I feel stupid! Not only were Nancy and her friend splitting my weekly paycheck to buy more drugs but I soon discovered that the secret silence I was supposed to be buying with my money had not been kept secret at all.

But it wasn't just a matter of silence. One night I received a phone call informing me that there was a contract out on my life. I didn't know how to get out of that mess. Because I was supporting Nancy's habit, she certainly wouldn't let me go. I couldn't call Mom and Dad because I couldn't stand to hear them say "I told you so." Finally I came to the realization that, although I was in a world of millions of people, I was totally alone. There was no one to turn to and even worse, no one who cared.

For some two hours I gazed into a mirror, evaluating my life and wondering how things could get so bad so quickly. I remembered witnessing the miracle-working power of God as a nine-year-old boy, only to have that followed by the physical abuse of a teacher I had trusted but who was trying to deal with his own pain. Event by event, I rehearsed my seventeen-year existence as tears dripped into the sink below. Questions haunted me: Is there any hope for me? Is there a future?

Then I was taken back to the best memory of my life—to that cellar door where I would lie looking at the mountains as they touched the sky, talking to God as to a friend. But would God listen to me after all I had been doing? After all, I hadn't been to church in a long time and the people in my new world were anything but Christian. Through the tears and the pain, I remember swallowing hard and saying just three words, "God, help me!"

I dropped the razor blade and heard it tinkle against the porcelain sink as I bowed over on the floor and began to weep. I had chosen not to kill myself but now was faced with the question of how I was going to live. After a few minutes, I rose from the floor, washed my face with cold water, and walked out of the house as if the whole incident had been a bad dream. As the cool air hit my face, I felt a strong urge to call my oldest sister, Jean. As the eldest in the family, maybe Jean would have some insight that could get me out of my situation.

When Jean answered the phone, I was amazed when she said, "Rick, it is so good to hear from you. I have been fasting and praying for you. You have been on my mind for weeks now." And then she invited me to come live with her. Somebody really cared! Somebody really wanted me! I was shocked, but gladly accepted her invitation.

Then I began to scramble to make arrangements to get to Jean's home more than 600 miles away. Getting there would take money. Then I remembered I had not yet picked up a $60 check at work. When I called the Greyhound bus station, I realized that my ticket would eat up most of that check, but I could make it if I snacked my way there. A plan seemed to be developing. Little did I realize how this one good decision would drastically affect my life. I climbed on the bus carrying a few clothes I had thrown into a suitcase while Nancy was away from home. I was on my way out of Texas, I hoped to something better. After a trip that should have taken ten hours but lasted twenty-one, I arrived in Murray, Kentucky, vowing never to ride a bus again.

I arrived at 7 a.m. on August 5, 1972, and at 2:05 p.m. that same day, Debbie Peal, a friend of my oldest niece, Donna, walked into Jean's house. Man, she was sharp! But I played it cool. As she said hello, I nodded, taking a draw off a freshly lit cigarette. Soon Donna emerged from her bedroom; she and Debbie waved goodbye and down the sidewalk they went toward the driveway. But something had happened to me in that brief encounter. For the twenty-one hours on the bus, I had prayed not for salvation or forgiveness, but rather that God would give me a Christian girl who would help me get my life straightened out. This Debbie Peal was certain to be an answer to my prayers.

About that time, Jean walked through the living room. "Hey, Jean," I said. "See that girl right there?"

Jean looked out the window where I was pointing and asked, "You mean Debbie?"

"Yeah, that's her," I said. "She's going to be my wife someday!"

Chuckling, Jean looked at me and said, "You are a moron!"

"I might be," I responded, "but that's Mrs. Moron right there." We both laughed and Jean continued on her way to the kitchen.

In a few moments, she returned to the living room, this time with a plan. She said, "Did you know, Rick, tomorrow there's a church youth camp that begins about twenty miles from here? Debbie will be there all week long, along with some 250 young men that don't know your future plans. Maybe you should go there and protect your interests." Her plan appeared reasonable to me, so Sunday afternoon I found myself heading off to church camp with Jean and her three teenage children. Jean had a career as a lunchroom manager and volunteered as the camp cook.

When I arrived, there were hundreds of teenagers between the ages of thirteen and twenty. I was nearly eighteen by this time and of course, much more mature concerning life—at least that was my opinion. Then I saw Debbie. I collected my thoughts and walked over to her. The first words out of my mouth were to offer her my class ring. I wanted to secure her loyalty before the competition began. Sure, I was messed up, but nothing was lacking concerning my confidence with the ladies! For some unknown reason, she accepted the ring. Now, we were going steady. So I leaned over and kissed her to seal the deal. Of course, that was against all rules, but what did I care—rules never meant much to me.

The news of our relationship quickly made its way around the camp. It motivated the camp leadership to prayer. Later they revealed that I had been the topic of discussion. Their only hope of having a peaceful camp, they agreed, was for "this boy to get saved."

Camp officially began at 7 p.m. Monday night with a service beginning with singing. There I sat, proudly perched on a back seat beside Debbie, trying to act cool and unconcerned. But as the service progressed, I found myself struggling to hold back tears. I could feel God reaching out to me. He had answered my prayers by moving me out of Texas, giving me Debbie and a new beginning, but I had not made one single change in my life for Him. Thought after thought concerning His love, His protection, and His mercy bombarded me. Finally, I decided that night would be a night of change.

Every time I looked up, it seemed that everyone in the building was looking at me. I could see their lips moving and I realized they were praying for me. Then came the real challenge. Could I make it until the invitation was given? The answer to that question was NO! At 7:35 p.m., I fell to the floor on my knees and asked Jesus to become the Lord of my life. The burden of sin was lifted from me, and when I looked up, I realized that the whole service had come to a halt. Everyone in the building had gathered around me; they were praying for me and crying with me. God was giving me the loving family I had longed for all my life.

That was the greatest day of my life. I was born again, a new creature, but yet my mind was still confused. Nothing had changed outwardly. Back in Dallas there was still a contract on my life, something Debbie knew nothing about. None of the people knew what my previous life had been. Some things you just can't tell people, can you?

That night was wonderful. One after another, people came to me with congratulations on my decision to follow Jesus. Over and over they whispered in my ear, "Brother Rick, now you need to start reading your Bible." "Easy for you to say!" I thought, knowing I hadn't read anything since elementary school, and even then I was the worst reader in my class. With everything in me I wanted to heed their advice, but in the days to follow I would only be filled with frustration over trying to read my Bible. I couldn't pronounce the names, nor could I make sense of how Bible reading was supposed to deliver me out of my pain. I felt somewhat like the disciples must have felt on the hillside with Jesus that day—it seemed more than was humanly possible.

After months of struggling with this issue, someone mentioned that the Bible was available on cassette tapes. I had never heard of such a thing. What a neat idea—listening while someone else read the Bible for me! I quickly bought a set of Bible tapes, put on my earphones, grabbed my Bible, and read along as Alexander Scorby read the Bible to me. Through his eloquent voice, I learned to pronounce those unpronounceable names. And through this daily exercise, I also learned to read. Until then there was no way that I would ever read anything aloud to people. But little by little, day by day, I began to feel the dignity that reading was releasing in me. I remember reading the Bible through three times in a year, not even fully aware of how it was renewing my mind and revolutionizing my life. I was becoming more and more aware of my need of learning.

About this time, Debbie's brother, Donnie, decided to attend a Bible college in Houston, Texas, and asked if I'd like to go along. I didn't want to leave Debbie, plus I was afraid that I really couldn't cut it in college. After all, I was just learning to read fluently, and I was sure that college would offer more challenges than I could handle. Besides those excuses, by that time God was really using my life. He had given me influence with approximately fifty young people who were looking to me for answers and for whom I felt responsible. I did realize that I needed more education but didn't know how to get it without going back to school.

One day as I listened to a teaching tape, the speaker made

a statement that dramatically impacted my life. He said, "A bachelor's degree is equivalent to the cumulative knowledge of fifty books on any particular subject." For example, someone with an engineering degree had knowledge equal to that of someone who had read fifty books on engineering or vice versa. There was my answer. I couldn't go to Bible college but I also didn't have to remain uneducated, for now I could read. I began my self-education by reading one book a month, then I went to two, then three. Eventually, I was reading fifty books a year, along with reading my Bible through year after year. My life was changed!

I believe there are two great decisions that will forever change your life. Of course, the greater of these is accepting Jesus Christ as your personal Savior. But the second great decision is to be a lifelong learner. There are many ways to receive an education: through academic institutions, through personal life experiences, and through reading about the experiences of others, just to name a few. Through reading, we are able to remain current with changing trends and technological advancements. Since information is expanding at an unprecedented pace, we must commit ourselves to read. Leaders are readers and readers are leaders. If you don't read, you will soon

> *LEADERS ARE READERS AND READERS ARE LEADERS. IF YOU DON'T READ, YOU WILL SOON BECOME YESTERDAY'S NEWS.*

become yesterday's news. The greatest revelation I discovered in all my years of ministry is that there are so many things yet to be learned! Volumes could be written about what I do not know. Therefore I must keep learning, learning as I am leading other learners up the mountain.

As I'm training leaders around the world, I'm often asked to reveal the keys to my success. I can think of countless lessons I believe are noteworthy and important and have summarized all of them into just three words that I want to share with you as I end this chapter on learning. I call them the Three Ps—prayer, personal development, and priority.

Prayer

The first P is Prayer. I have never met a great man or woman of God who was not also a person of prayer. Since only God knows the future, we must become people of prayer if we hope to discern our next step. Prayer is not something we do before we work, prayer is the work! Every leader should develop a prayer list. Included on that list should be our family members, those to whom we are responsible, and those for whom we are responsible. I personally believe God will never give us the responsibility to develop leaders if we are unwilling to pray for them daily. We demonstrate our commitment through our daily prayer life.

Jesus gave us the example to follow. He went from one place of prayer to the next place of prayer, and in between He performed miracles. As the disciples witnessed His life of power and love, their request was simple: "Lord, teach us to pray" (Luke 11:1). Notice they didn't ask the Lord to teach them to preach, or teach, or work miracles, but instead to teach them to pray. They completely understood that the key to power was found in learning to pray! The same is true today. If Jesus needed to pray to carry out His work, how could we hope to do the work without prayer? Establish a prayer list now, and commit yourself to be a person of prayer.

Personal Development

The second P is Personal Development. When I speak of personal development, I'm referring to reading and studying. Leaders should have a plan, an ongoing plan, to improve their skills and hone their gifts. Without a specific plan and time set aside, we often find ourselves the victims of a busy schedule, with no time for the most important things. I know many leaders who have what I refer to as a "someday mentality." Someday they're going to read that book or research that subject, but at the end of a string of "somedays" they discover that life has passed them by. It is never too late to learn and today is the day to begin.

My suggestion is that you read books consistent with your gifts. Dr. Peter Wagner has an excellent tool available to help you to discover your Spiritual gifts—the Wagner-Modified Houts Questionaire. I used it to discover my spiritual gifts. Now my educational reading is focused on the five areas of my spiritual gifts: relationships, missions, prayer, leadership, and spiritual gifts.

You will become what you are preparing to become, so start today!

Priority

The third P is Priority. This one will make or break you. If you are unable or unwilling to set priorities and protect them, be assured that you will never reach your maximum potential. A number of things will constantly vie for your attention and it will be difficult to make the proper decision between what is urgent and what is truly important. People will add to your frustration by placing demands and expectations on you as well. You can find yourself constantly busy with little or no visible progress. Priority is necessary for true progress.

I believe the Bible offers the best guide for developing proper priorities for your life. First priority must be your personal relationship with Jesus Christ.

The second priority is you. It is easy to overlook our need for exercise, for rest and relaxation, and for personal reflection. Often our most neglected area is ourselves.

Third priority is our family. First was God, then Adam, then came Eve, then Cain and Abel, so our family must hold their proper place on our priority list. For too long families have been destroyed because ministers have put their ministries ahead of their families. Don't lose your family while trying to save the world!

Fourth is the universal body of believers. In Matthew 16:18, Jesus said, "Upon this rock I will build my church." We must hold in high regard the church of the Lord Jesus Christ.

Fifth is the local body of believers. I believe everyone should be faithfully involved in a local church and under the authority of a local pastor.

The sixth priority encompasses our spiritual gifts and ministry to the Body of Christ.

Keeping our priorities in proper Biblical order will allow us to experience the fullness of what God desires for our lives. But if we allow our priorities to get out of order, we will indeed suffer loss.

As we make our way down the mountain after learning this lesson, don't forget that learning is not just an experience but rather is a lifestyle. We must implement the truth, for only the applied truth will bring change. Never stop growing and giving of yourself to help others grow. The whole purpose of the Mountain of Instruction is the valley below, for in the valley is where we have the opportunity to help fellow travelers on their way to the top. There is always a higher plane of learning, so keep learning!

WHEN JESUS THEN LIFTED UP HIS EYES, AND SAW A GREAT COMPANY COME UNTO HIM, HE SAITH UNTO PHILIP, "WHENCE SHALL WE BUY BREAD, THAT THESE MAY EAT?" (JOHN 6:5)

"Wow," the disciple Philip must have thought, "a field trip! Everything has been so hectic since we started following Jesus. Certainly He must realize how tired we are. After all, none of us has ever been involved in full-time ministry before."

Everything was perfect—the mountainside setting near the Sea of Tiberias was miles from the nearest city. This mountain was not far from the mountain where Jesus delivered the Beatitudes, so the terrain was familiar, but the disciples had never before been to that specific spot. They must have been ecstatic over the thought of finally getting a day of rest and relaxation with Jesus. They had no idea that their planned getaway would quickly change to an unplanned crusade.

Word quickly spread that Jesus was near and a multitude gathered with one common goal in mind—to get their needs met. They had brought with them their sick, their lame, and their demon-possessed family and friends. This was their one chance to be touched by Jesus and they were determined to not let Him pass them by. Desperation overrode any reservations they may have held about intruding into a private meeting between Jesus and His twelve. One thing was certain; they knew that Jesus loved them and that He would forgive them of any customs or traditions they may have violated.

Literally thousands of people gathered around them on the hillside and in the valley below. Jesus ministered to them, teaching, healing the sick, and casting out devils. It was amazing to watch! But before long, the disciples grew weary. Minutes turned into hours, and before you could say "Beersheba," the whole day was gone. So much for the private time they had anticipated! Stomachs were growling all around as everyone struggled to stay focused on what Jesus was saying.

The disciples were no different than those in the crowd; they too had become hungry and tired, battling their flesh and thinking to themselves, "When is this meeting going to end?" Perhaps they question ed why Jesus didn't simply dismiss the people and send them to their homes. After all, Passover was nearing and the people needed to prepare for their journeys to Jerusalem. "Perfect solution," the disciples may have thought, "just dismiss them. They'll understand."

But Jesus had another idea. He leaned over to Philip and whispered, "Philip, where can we buy bread to feed all these people?"

Philip was shocked at the very suggestion of such a thing and must have thought to himself, "Jesus, you must be joking. We're in the middle of nowhere. Can you imagine how much it would cost to feed this crowd? And even if we had the money, no local eatery could cater such an event as this. Let's be reasonable, Jesus, there must be at least twenty thousand people here!"

About that time, Andrew reported the reality of the situation. "I've searched high and low, and all we can come up with is a little boy's lunch, five small barley loaves and two little fish. But what good will that do us for such a crowd as this?" The disciples waited in suspense for Jesus' response, surely believing they had convinced Him of the impossibility they were facing. They were likely also convinced Jesus would now make the decision to send the people home.

But Jesus made a shocking announcement, "Have the people sit down in an orderly fashion and prepare for supper." Stunned, the disciples followed His instruction, even while thinking the food would soon run out and lots of people would be disappointed. But, Jesus took their humble offering and lifted it toward Heaven, giving thanks to the Father. He blessed it and broke it, and then gave it to the disciples for distribution.

Let's not read into this story more than what the Bible actually says. Nowhere is it recorded that Jesus multiplied the bread and the fish, but rather that He blessed it, broke it, and gave it to His disciples for distribution. Can you imagine their bewilderment? Though reluctant to question Jesus further, still they must have thought, "What are we supposed to do with this?" So the disciples went to the first person and offered the fish and the bread. It was at that moment that multiplication occurred!

This is one of the most important principles I've learned concerning Kingdom provision, but it comes much later in sequence. So let's leave it there for now and we'll get back to it later. First, though, let me share with you what I've learned as I've journeyed with Jesus through the mountains and valleys of my own life.

The date was April 18, 1975, our wedding day. What a marvelous occasion! Debbie and I were both twenty years old, wide-eyed and innocent, the youngest in our families but raised in vastly different homes. Our expectations could not have been more different, though our love for each other was the same. The church was packed with our families and friends as the clock ticked toward 6:30 p.m. Then the moment we had dreamed of arrived.

The church was beautifully decorated and everyone was dressed in their best, I noted as I walked out of a side door and took my place next to our pastor, the Reverend Paul D. Wanger. The back doors of the church opened, and the music of "The Wedding March" began. Debbie made her entrance, taking her place alongside me at the front of the church. To the question, "Who giveth this woman to be wed to this man?" Debbie's father responded, placing her hand in mine. The congregation was quiet and I listened carefully to the words of our pastor as he went through the vows. He spoke of two becoming one. Even though the words were penetrating my ears, honestly I was waiting for my cue. I didn't want to miss those two important words, "I do!"

Everything went off without a hitch. It was beautiful. I kissed my bride, never realizing the struggles that would follow as we tried to live out our "I dos." To be truthful, Debbie and I started marriage with the same idea—we would change each other into seeing things our way. Our expectations would soon crash head-on.

Debbie had lived in a family that operated under a budget, and at the top of that budget was their tithe. In contrast, I didn't even know what a budget was. In my family, we were just happy to be eating! I had been raised in a coal mining camp where the company owned everything—the house we lived in, the grocery store, the clothing store, the gas station, and much more. Those who worked for the company charged what they needed to their company account. When payday came, my dad's check was applied toward his company bill and he received a few coins in return. There simply wasn't a lot of money to worry about.

Maybe you remember the old song "Sixteen Tons" written by Merle Travis and made famous by singer Tennessee Ernie Ford. There's a line in that song that says, "I owe my soul to the company store." That line must have been written about the Clendenen family! With so many kids, Mom and Dad were never able to pay off their company bill. It was almost like being raised in a communist country in which nothing is individually owned, but the individual's most basic needs are supplied. This was not the best arrangement, but at least Dad and Mom were able to feed all of us and I'm not certain they could have done that without such a system.

Even after the government broke up the company's monopoly, my parents struggled to handle money and to feed all of us. One thing my father refused to do was tithe. He had convinced himself that it was not Biblical. His belief was that the preacher should work just like he did. Dad had a strong work ethic and his favorite saying was, "If a man doesn't work, he shouldn't eat." So, the preacher and the church weren't getting his money.

On the other hand, Debbie's family was completely different. Her father was a preacher, had pastored a church, and had strong convictions concerning tithing and church support. Her family realized the blessings that accompanied giving.

The battle lines in our family were drawn. I was sure that my Mom and Dad had it right and Debbie was just as sure her parents were correct. The only difference was that Debbie seemed to have the Bible on her side of the argument.

Although I could win an argument against Debbie, I found I couldn't win against the Bible. The Word of God and the visible blessings on Debbie's family started me on a journey to discover for myself what the Bible had to say about money and about financial blessings.

Over the years I have discovered a number of principles that have revolutionized my thinking and have positioned me for blessings. The most important thing I've discovered is the mercy of God as He gently led me step by step along this process, forgiving my stubbornness and mistakes and revealing the next piece of the puzzle.

RELATIONAL HONORING

The principles I have learned are really not as much about money as they are about relational honoring. As I share these principles with you, let me encourage you not to judge yourself too harshly for any mistakes you may have made. Instead, please realize that God is a God of process and all of us go through seasons in our lives. My hope is that these principles will bring you into a harvest season that will result in a greater level of blessing as well as Kingdom advancement.

> *...GOD IS A GOD OF PROCESS AND ALL OF US GO THROUGH SEASONS IN OUR LIVES.*

Principle 1: Tithing is a Principle of Relationship, Not Law

I discovered that, in contrast to what I had been taught, the concept of tithing did not originate in Malachi 3:10 where it says: "Bring ye all the tithes into the storehouse, that there may be meat in mine house, and prove me now herewith, saith the

Lord of hosts, if I will not open you the windows of heaven, and pour you out a blessing, that there shall not be room enough to receive it." Instead I discovered that Adam and Eve tithed and taught their children to tithe as well. As I learned more, I realized that hundreds of years before Moses and the Law, Abraham tithed; and Jacob promised to tithe during the time he was running for his life. These pre-law examples seemed to indicate that tithing is a principle of relationship and not one of law.

This is without doubt the most important principle I have learned concerning the provision of God. When Debbie first brought up our need to tithe, I perceived tithing as a legalistic action, an obligation that I was forced to fulfill to be a good Christian. Remember, I was twenty years old at that time, struggling to be the head of my house. I wasn't going to be forced to do anything. And like my dad, I couldn't see a New Testament scripture that demanded me to do such a thing. Therefore, to me, it was optional. But I began to notice that week after week, month after month, things happened to eat up the very money that I was trying to save by not tithing.

Finally, I decided to give tithing a try. I was a long way from being a cheerful giver, but I discovered that God accepts tithe from the grouchy as well! Even then, He blessed us and showed Himself faithful to us. We could see the fruit in our lives as God proved Himself to us that we might, in turn, move into a deeper relationship with Him.

My view about tithing began to change. Suddenly it was no longer about tithing or even money, for that matter; instead the question was about honor. Was I willing to honor God and our relationship with my substance? Tithing and giving was just a means of revealing my love and honor to God, recognizing

Him as my source and supply. It was to be an expression of love and thanksgiving for the relationship we enjoyed. I began to regard and refer to our giving as "relational honoring."

It is apparent from the lives of the children of Adam and Eve that God taught their parents the need for "relational honoring." Long before Noah, Abraham, or Moses and the Law, the first mention of tithing is found in the story of Cain and Abel: "And in process of time it came to pass, that Cain brought of the fruit of the ground an offering unto the Lord. And Abel, he also brought of the firstlings of his flock and of the fat thereof. And the LORD had respect unto Abel and to his offering" (Genesis 4:3–4).

The two eldest sons of Adam and Eve understood that God was their source and provider. Therefore, giving back to Him was recognition of their relationship with Him. This story teaches us not only the importance of honoring our relationship with God, but it is equally important how we honor that relationship. In that I discovered the second principle.

Principle 2: Honor is Attached Only to the First

For years I tithed without realizing the importance of the first fruit. I had often heard it preached that Cain's offering was rejected because it was not of blood, but rather of fruit and grain while Abel's offering was accepted because it was of blood. But that explanation never seemed to fit. As I read the Bible for myself, I could see throughout scripture that God accepted fruit and grain as an offering, and even Jesus Himself commended the religious leaders of His day for tithing of the grains, anise and cummin. So, I thought, there must be something else being taught by the story of the sacrifices offered by Cain and Abel.

It was then that I discovered the second principle. The distinction between Cain's offering and Abel's was found in the opening statement in verse 3: "And *in process of time* it came to pass, that Cain brought... an offering..." (emphasis added) and in verse 4, "And Abel, he also brought of the *firstlings* of his flock..." (emphasis added). Revelation hit me then—it is not only important what you do concerning tithe, but when you do it.

For years I tithed but I did it "in the process of time." When I got my check on Fridays I paid the car payment, bought groceries, and paid bills. Then Sunday morning, "in the process of time," we pulled out our checkbook and paid our tithe. All along Debbie and I thought that was acceptable to God, but we also wondered why we were not walking in the fullness of blessing. Tithing is a relational principle and is meant to show honor to God, so it is very important to give God the first.

Even the natural world teaches us the importance of this principle. If you invite someone to your home for cake and coffee, you refer to him as a guest of honor. With him seated at your table, and with the cake sliced and ready to serve, whom do you serve first and why? Naturally, you serve the first to your guest. Why? To show him the honor that is due him as the honored guest in your home. Doesn't God deserve that same honor?

Proverbs 3:9 commands us to bring the first: "Honour the Lord with thy substance, and with the firstfruits of all thine increase..." Leviticus 27:30 (NKJV) says: "And all the tithe of the land, whether of the seed of the land, or of the fruit of the tree, is the Lord's. It is holy to the Lord."

Not only is it important to God what you do, but why you do it and when you do it. These particular scriptures lead us to our third and fourth principles.

Principle 3: Tithing is a Test

The word tithe means tenth. Why would God require the first 10 percent of our income instead of 3 percent, or 7 percent, or 12 percent? After all, three, seven, and twelve are all significant Biblical numbers. God requires the first 10 percent because ten is His number of testing. As you read the Bible, you'll discover Jacob's wages were changed ten times to test his love for Rachel. There were ten plagues in Egypt to test Pharaoh's heart. Ten commandments were given to Israel to test their commitment to God. Job's "comforters" spoke to him ten times in what became a test of his faithfulness to God. Nehemiah's commitment was tested by ten negative statements made against him. In one of Jesus' parables, ten virgins were tested in what was a lesson on preparedness.

Over and over in scripture we see that the number ten is connected to testing. Could it be that in tithing God tests our relationship with Him, discovering whether we have Him as the top priority in our lives? After all, the Bible teaches that the first belongs to the Lord. We find this in Exodus 13:1–2: "And the LORD spake unto Moses, saying, Sanctify unto me all the firstborn, whatsoever openeth the womb among the children of Israel, [both] of man and of beast: it [is] mine." Can God trust us to honor our relationship with Him by returning what already belongs to Him?

Back when I wasn't tithing I became offended when people would say that I was robbing God, even though that was the question God Himself asked in Malachi 3:8: "Will a man rob

God?..." Since it was my money, I couldn't see how I was robbing God. Now I realize that the money wasn't mine. The first belongs to God and if you keep what belongs to someone else, even if you're not being called a thief, you are a thief.

So the test was simple. Could I be trusted with what belonged to God? Would I honor Him by returning to Him the first of what He had so graciously given to me? And could I pass the test, the test to be blessed? And would I tithe first or in the process of time?

Principle 4: Ten is the Number of Redemption

Not only is ten the number of testing, but it is also the number of redemption. As we return to God the first of all of our increase, He receives it as an act of honor. That act of honor begins a redemptive process that results in true Biblical prosperity for Kingdom advancement.

The law of redemptive effect is found in Leviticus 27:30 and Exodus 13:12–13. I have already made references to Leviticus 27 and Exodus 13, and I encourage you to read these chapters on your own. But let me summarize what they are saying:

By returning the first fruits of your increase to God, a transformation takes place in what remains. Exodus 13 tells us that the first is given to redeem. For example, the unclean had to be redeemed by what was clean. A lamb had to be sacrificed to redeem a donkey; one animal was considered clean, the other unclean. This is such an important truth. God redeems our finances from a corrupt world system by deeming our first fruits, the tenth, as holy. This is found in Leviticus 27:30. Once we give the first 10 percent to God, and it is received by Him as an act of honor and is deemed holy, then it can redeem the 90 percent that remains, changing the spirit that is attached to our finances.

It is important to understand that all money has a spirit attached to it. All of us want the Spirit of God to rest upon our finances.

We discover this in Luke chapter 16 as Jesus Himself says that you cannot worship God and mammon. Most translators merely translate mammon as money. But mammon was actually a Syrian word that described a demonic deity or god. This demon god was well-known in the Middle Ages by a variety of names. The Syrians called him Mammon, the Romans called him Dis Pater, the Greeks called him Plutus. But in every case, he personified the love of money by offering the riches of this world without justice or morality. God has another plan altogether, and that plan offers true prosperity by doing what is right. There is a way to redeem our finances from a world system of corruption to a Kingdom place of blessing.

So tithing is much more than proving our faithfulness to God and to our relationship with Him. Tithing also teaches us Kingdom principles that will lead to the blessing of God in true prosperity.

Principle 5: It All Belongs to God

Even after learning these valuable principles, something was still missing. Debbie and I were struggling to make ends meet and were living from paycheck to paycheck with no evidence of multiplication in our lives. I became so frustrated! Even though I had been tithing for years, I became convinced that it didn't work for everyone. I considered that perhaps I was just a bad manager or made bad financial decisions. I knew the Word of God was true, so I believed I must have done something to sabotage my own financial future.

One day as I was praying (or should I say grumbling?) on my

knees, I said, "Lord, I am trying to trust you with my finances." It was then that God lovingly rebuked me with a startling response, "What do you mean trust Me with your finances? I've been twenty years trying to trust you with my Kingdom. If I could trust you, I would release Kingdom provision to you."

I was stunned! I had been taught that He received the first 10 percent and I assumed that the remaining 90 percent belonged to me. How wrong I was. Scripture tells us in Psalm 24:1: "The earth is the Lord's, and the fullness thereof; the world, and they that dwell therein."

This revelation led me to a scripture that had caused me great concern over the years. In fact, I had avoided this scripture because of my lack of understanding. It is found in Luke 16:1–13 and is known as the story of the unjust steward. I'm sure you are familiar with the story. The steward is about to lose his job so he goes to those who owe his master money and he reduces what they owe. He reasons that by doing so, after he loses his job he'll still have some friends to whom he can turn. Through the words spoken by the master in the parable, Jesus commends the unjust steward, saying that he is wiser than the children of light. Was Jesus commending his crookedness? The answer is certainly no. But he does use his actions to teach us three things we need to understand as stewards in the Kingdom of God.

First, He says in verse 9 to make friends of unrighteous mammon. In saying this, Jesus is not promoting the love of money but rather the enhancing of relationships. Every relationship is like a piggy bank—its value is equal to its investment. Jesus commends the unjust steward because He has valued relationships with people higher than money itself.

Secondly Jesus says, "Therefore if you have not been faithful in unrighteous mammon, who will commit to your trust the true riches?" (verse 11, NJKV) The lesson to be learned here is how we handle money is a test of whether or not God can release to us the Kingdom provision. How can I faithfully handle unrighteous mammon? Here's how: By redeeming the firstfruits, through the redemptive process of tithing, and then faithfully using what remains to carry out the will of the Master.

Finally, in verse 12 (NKJV) we read: "And if you have not been faithful in what is another man's, who will give you what is your own?" I had been waiting for years for God to discover my faithfulness in tithing but He had been waiting for years for me to realize that I was not an owner, but rather a steward. God will not promote an owner. Promotion is given to those who recognize they are stewards, and stewards only, of the Kingdom of God. Although it all belongs to Him—the 10 percent and the 90 percent—not one time had I asked Him what I was to do with the ninety. That was my problem. If I was proven faithful as a steward, God promised to promote me.

Principle 6: Blessing is in His Hands; Multiplication is in Ours

Now we are ready to return to Jesus and His disciples on the hillsides of Galilee. In spite of Jesus' blessing, the disciples could not see how five small loaves and two fish would feed a multitude. There was no visible increase. In the physical realm, things looked exactly the same, but in the spiritual realm, everything had changed. By placing what they had in the hands of Jesus, it was blessed and now carried the potential of multiplication. Jesus was teaching them an important principle: Multiplication occurs when you take what is blessed and distribute it to those whom God desires to bless.

This was exam time for the disciples. Would they approach this massive crowd strictly on the word of Jesus? Would they honor Him and His desire? That was also the question facing me. I had learned to release the 10 percent to Him, but I was holding firmly to the 90 percent. Would I give Him everything? I decided that the answer was yes, I would become trustworthy; I would redeem through tithing the 10 percent and then I would consult Him concerning the remainder.

> *MULTIPLICATION OCCURS WHEN YOU TAKE WHAT IS BLESSED AND DISTRIBUTE IT TO THOSE WHOM GOD DESIRES TO BLESS.*

Principle 7: Multiplication is a Result of Relational Honoring

Finally I understood! Everything belongs to God. As a faithful steward, I must consult Him on what I am to do with everything He has placed in my hands. This was altogether a new thought for me that brought up other questions. I realized that if tithing reflects a relational principle, then there must be something I was missing in connection with the 90 percent, something concerning other relationships. But what?

That question started me on a study concerning honor. If tithing is how I honor God, should I also honor other relationships, and how should I honor them? Was this what He was trying to teach me? Yes! I discovered that we are commanded to honor a variety of relationships. We are told:

1. As servants we are to honor God with our firstfruits – Proverbs 3:9

2. As sons, we are to honor our fathers – Malachi 1:6

3. As servants (employees) we are to honor our masters (employers) – Malachi 1:6
4. As children we are to honor our mothers and fathers – Ephesians 6:2
5. As church members we are to give double honor to spiritual leaders – 1 Timothy 5:17
6. As husbands we are to honor our wives – 1 Peter 3:7
7. As citizens we are to honor our governmental leaders – Romans 13:7
8. As spiritual leaders we are to honor one another – Romans 12:10
9. As members of the Body of Christ we are to honor the lowly – 1 Corinthians 12:23
10. As Christians, we are to honor all men and honor the king – 1 Peter 2:17

Money is, of course, just one way we show honor. But certainly, money reflects our honor. As I began to pray about this, it became quite evident that God truly wanted to control my financial decisions. So I asked Him, "Lord, what do you want me to do first?"

I don't think I have ever received such a quick response from God. He said, "I want you to give double honor to your spiritual fathers."

"Lord," I asked, "are you talking about money here?" Again He affirmed that He was. I turned to 1 Timothy 5:18 and discovered, indeed, that it was talking about money as it says not to "muzzle the ox that is treading out the corn. And, the labourer is worthy of his reward."

Then the question became evident, double what? I felt the Lord was telling me to give to my spiritual leaders double the tithe I was giving to Him. Since I had three spiritual fathers in my life, 20% to each, plus my regular 10% tithe would be 70% of my income. Surely that couldn't be the case. But the more I prayed about it, the more I felt this was the direction of God for our lives. So Debbie and I decided to obey God, though it seemed impossible. To say that a miracle took place would be the understatement of all time. God literally opened Heaven over us and multiplication began to take place in our lives.

As multiplication continued, God began to lead us to honor other relationships. Each time we followed the command of the Lord, multiplication increased, allowing us to invest in more and more relationships. It was then that the Lord spoke a statement to me that I have held close for years, "There is no shortage in the Kingdom of God except of obedience and honor."

I can assure you, my friend, that what I am saying here is not some get-rich-quick scheme. Nor is it a way for us to gain and hoard the things this world has to offer. But I can tell you for sure that it is an avenue for promotion in the Kingdom of God. As we prove ourselves faithful stewards of Kingdom provision, God will allow us to become instruments of Kingdom advancement.

So, let's go back to the disciples on the mountainside and what happened after the miracle. Thousands of people were fed, a little boy received twelve baskets full of fish and bread as interest on his lunch, and people were shouting, wanting to make Jesus king. But for the answer to what happened next, let's look at John 6:15: "When Jesus therefore perceived that they would come and take him by force, to make him a king, he departed again into a mountain himself alone."

Are you ready to go higher up the mountain—above materialism, above position, above so-called prosperity, and even above miracles? Are you ready to follow Jesus higher than you've ever been before so that you may see things from His Kingdom perspective? If the answer is yes, then gather up your gear and start climbing to where He has gone, for He is alone and awaiting your arrival.

CHAPTER 5 | MOUNTAIN OF GLORY

AND AFTER SIX DAYS JESUS TAKETH WITH HIM PETER, AND JAMES, AND JOHN, AND LEADETH THEM UP INTO AN HIGH MOUNTAIN APART BY THEMSELVES: AND HE WAS TRANSFIGURED BEFORE THEM. (MARK 9:2)

The setting for this lesson, the Bible says, was a high mountain. Taking place just six days after the feeding of the four thousand, what was to be learned on this mountain was no normal teaching. Separating this lesson from previous lessons was the fact that only those with special invitation could attend. Not an open forum, this was a private retreat for the inner circle, those closest to Jesus. In fact, what took place on this mountain could not even be shared with the other disciples, let alone the multitude.

In mentoring others, I've come to understand that there are different levels of intimacy that I refer to as the five levels of leadership influence. To describe them I use the biblical number examples of one, three, twelve, seventy, and multitude. Here's what I mean: God had an intimate relationship and leadership influence with one in Abraham; then He expanded that to three in reference to Abraham, Isaac and Jacob; expanding His leadership influence further, He included the twelve sons of Jacob; then He encompassed the seventy who journeyed to Egypt during famine; and finally, a multitude came out of Egypt.

Look at this in the life of Moses and you'll see the same numeric principles. Moses and God had an intimate one-on-

one relationship; in turn, Moses had Hur, Aaron and Joshua; there were twelve spies, each representing one of the twelve tribes of Israel; Moses appointed seventy elders; and Moses was the leader of a multitude.

The same is true in the ministry of Jesus Christ. First, Jesus had John, His closest follower, known as The Beloved, the one who laid his head upon His chest, the one who knew His heartbeat; then came the inner circle of Peter, James and John; after that were the twelve disciples; then the seventy disciples; and finally the multitude.

It is very important to understand that a spiritual leader cannot be intimate with a multitude. Instead, one's greatest eternal impact occurs within a smaller, more intimate, circle of followers. This explains why Jesus often sent the multitude away in order to spend time with the twelve.

> *ONE'S GREATEST ETERNAL IMPACT OCCURS WITHIN A SMALLER, MORE INTIMATE, CIRCLE OF FOLLOWERS.*

Now back to the setting of this chapter's text. Jesus was on a mountaintop with His inner circle, Peter, James and John. The lesson of the day would be life changing.

As Peter, James and John focused intently on Jesus, He became infused and saturated with the glory of God. His clothing was whiter than white, and He glowed as if a light emanated from within Him. As they watched in stunned silence, Moses and Elijah appeared beside Jesus and began to talk with Him. Can you imagine what the three disciples must have thought? Not even their wildest dreams compared to what they were seeing. Even though they didn't understand the full meaning of what was happening, one thing was certain, they were involved in a holy moment they never wanted to forget.

It's easy for us now to look back and to criticize Peter for the statement he made in that sacred moment. But just think for a moment how you would have responded had you been there. To paraphrase Mark 9:5, Peter said, "This is wonderful. Why don't we build three shrines—one for you, Jesus, one for Moses and one for Elijah." The scripture explains the reason for Peter's response was that the disciples were terrified and didn't know what to say.

If that weren't enough, a cloud formed overhead and a thundering voice came from the cloud saying, "This is My beloved Son, listen to Him" (Mark 9:7). Any lingering doubts as to what was happening were immediately erased. The disciples knew they had just heard the audible voice of God the Father, and they also knew for sure that Jesus was exactly who He said—the Son of the living God!

Then suddenly, Moses, Elijah, and the cloud disappeared. Jesus turned to them and said, "Don't tell anyone what you have seen until I have been resurrected from the dead" (Mark 9:9). The Bible goes on to say that while the three disciples did keep the experience to themselves, they also asked each other, "What does all this mean?"

Each of us stands in need of God's stamp of approval upon our ministry. God spoke out of Heaven three times during the ministry of Jesus Christ. First, at Jesus' baptism, God the Father confirmed the man. Then later at the Mount of Transfiguration, God the Father confirmed the message of Jesus. Then finally, as recorded in John 12:27–28, God spoke a third time to confirm the mission of Jesus. Only God can confirm the man, the message, and the mission of our lives. Men can give affirmation, but only

God can give confirmation.

Many times, due to our insecurities, we value man's affirmation too greatly. We end up exchanging the confirmation of God for the affirmation of man, and in doing so become people pleasers. We want so much to hear words of approval that if we're not careful, we can end up feeding our need through the compliments of people whom God has called us to feed. Our responsibility is to please God, to serve God, and to focus on His confirmation rather than man's affirmation.

In writing these words it is difficult not to rehearse the mistakes I've made in my own life and ministry. Being raised as I was and constantly seeking affirmation from my father (by the way, I never received it), I found that I, too, became a people pleaser. Seeking to make everyone happy while being miserable myself, I went to extremes to avoid conflict. The result was that I experienced a lot of heartache in ministry.

I accepted God's call to preach in 1974. The first ten years of my preaching career can be characterized by one word—fear! I was afraid of failure, I was afraid of disappointing anyone, and I was afraid to use the word "no" when asked to do something. Therefore, I was always exhausted, frustrated, and overbooked, with little time for my family or anyone else. I felt like a donkey always trying to reach a carrot dangling before him on a stick. True success was always out of reach, and I was in desperate need for a word from God.

One Saturday afternoon in 1984 I was on my way to our church, desperately trying to keep up with the rigors of my self-inflicted schedule. Although I had never been a senior pastor, I was actively involved in ministry within the church. I lived a super busy life, working a forty hour work week, time that was coupled with over one hundred hours each month of voluntary ministry at the church. I was a sports addict as well, playing softball on two different leagues while squeezing in golf, tennis, bowling, and more. And did I mention that I also had a wife and two children whom I saw occasionally? As I walked down the aisle of our little country church, I had no idea God had called a meeting with me for that afternoon.

The church was dim, with the only light in the auditorium coming from a fluorescent light behind a wooden cross on the front wall. As I glanced toward that cross and felt my eyes and attention drawn to it, I heard the Spirit of the Lord speak clearly to my spirit and He asked, "When are you going to work for Me?"

I was baffled by the question. "Work for You?" I responded, "But, Lord, I hold some ten positions in this church. I'm involved in everything that is going on here. What do You mean, work for You?"

But then He replied with a sobering truth, "You're not doing this for Me. You're doing this for yourself that through the work of your hands you might receive the approval of men and feed the insecurity of your soul."

I broke into tears and crumpled into a pile on the floor. There in the second pew of that church, I realized that my labor had been in vain. Every word the Lord had spoken was true. My need for approval was so big that I would have done anything in the world to get it, including using God and ministry to scratch the itch I felt deep within my heart. I sobbed and repented, asking Him to forgive me. And as sad as it is to say, I admit that was the first time in ten years that I seriously asked Him to define His will for my life.

As He began to speak to me, every word was a challenge. I am not sharing what God told me with you in any belief that it is an answer for others who find themselves paddling their own ministry boat. Rather, it was a specific word for me at a specific time in my life. God said to me, "Resign every position you hold immediately and seek My face for further instruction."

Feeling panic's grip, I swallowed hard and wondered what everyone would think. I wondered what the pastor of the church would say. And all those people I had worked so hard to impress—would they criticize me, label me a quitter? Would they even understand or believe that I had truly heard from God?

The reality is that not everyone was supportive of my decision to resign my positions. Some did label me a quitter while other tried to talk me out of my "so-called" word from God. But in my spirit I knew God was calling me to a new level of accountability under His leadership.

Every day for the next week when I left my job in the afternoon I headed straight for the church. Since I didn't want to be seen and be placed in the position of explaining myself over and over to people who were unwilling to accept my decision, I hid my car behind the church building. Day after day I lay with my face on the ground, seeking God for hours at a time. Ashamed that I had used God and ministry for personal gratification, I felt lower than the dirt on which I was lying.

My prayer was simple. It may even have sounded humorous had passers-by heard, but God knew I meant it from the bottom of my heart. Over and over I cried, "God, please use my life. Anoint me. I don't care what you want me to do. Even if you want me to pick bubble gum off the bottom of the pews, I'll do my very best to be the best bubble gum picker You have ever called. Just please, anoint my life."

Looking back, I see that as a turning point. We serve a God who offers second chances, but how God led me was even more humbling than I could have imagined. He led me to clean the church bathrooms, mow the church yard, change light bulbs, remove spider webs, and other equally humbling tasks. Suddenly I found myself the new unpaid, unannounced, unnoticed, and misunderstood janitor of the church. But as I moved in obedience, I discovered God in a new way. As a servant, I discovered the joy of cleaning His toilet, mowing His yard, and changing the light bulbs in His house. And along with this joy, I discovered an anointing that was available regardless of the job I was doing, as long as what I did was for Him and was done with the pure heart of a servant. During that special time in my life I came to realize that Kingdom success is not found in the positions or titles we hold, but is truly defined by the servant heart within.

At the time, I was clueless that God was at work preparing me for His future plan. In 1979, God had used Joyce Meyer, who was virtually unknown at the time, to prophecy what God and God alone would bring to pass. The prophecy was as follows: "God is preparing for you a city that you know not of. But when the time is right, you will know that it is God and He will bless you there in a mighty way."

To be honest, I had nearly forgotten about that prophetic word and had no desire to go anywhere. But from the time of my 1984 Saturday afternoon encounter with God in an empty church until the summer of 1987, I was headed nowhere on a treadmill of ministry. All I knew was that God was at work, that He was changing my vision, and was moving me away from where I was. Like Abraham, I didn't know where I was going.

During those three years I received a number of ministry invitations. One invitation came from Michigan, another from Illinois, and there were several local opportunities for full-time ministry. But each time, I clearly heard God say no. So, after declining each invitation I returned to my volunteer position at the church and my full-time job driving a forklift at the Fisher-Price Toy Company plant where I had worked for nearly fifteen years. Everyone who worked with me there had grown tired of hearing about my desire to be in full-time ministry, and to be honest, I, too, was wondering if things would ever change. But change was just around the corner.

In May of 1987, I received a call from a ministry friend of mine. He told me a church congregation in Texas was looking for a pastor and that he had given them my name. I quickly told him that I was not interested and recited the negative experience of my youth in the Dallas area. Ending with how I hated Texas and never again wanted to go to there, I added, "You should have called me before you told those people I was interested. Call them back and tell them, 'Thanks, but no thanks!'" I hung up the phone and thought that was the end of it. Later my friend told me that God would not let him call the church leaders with my message.

So I was surprised when I received a telephone call from the chairman of the pulpit committee of People's Chapel in Perryton, Texas. After mentioning my friend's name he asked if I would consider making a trip to Texas to look at the church. I was anything but gracious in my response, and blurted out travel demands that I expected would put him off. Instead, I was surprised when he said, "That's perfect, Brother Clendenen. The tickets will be in the mail this week."

Stunned, and after agreeing to be there the second Sunday of May, I hung up the phone. His description of the church was nothing like what I thought I wanted. I was thirty-three years old then and the average age of the twenty-seven member congregation was somewhere in the mid-sixties. Plus, pastors of that congregation typically lasted no longer than a year and three months. The situation seemed more like a pastoral graveyard than an opportunity for a rookie to try his pastoral wings.

Thoughts of the upcoming visit put me on my face before God. Seeking confirmation, I "put out a fleece" before the Lord. "If you want me to go there, I'll go," I told Him. "But, please, if I am to become the pastor there, save someone the Sunday morning I am scheduled to preach there." Breathing a sigh of relief, I left my prayer believing that certainly no sinner would be drawn to a little church of elderly saints. But I was wrong.

Debbie and I were treated wonderfully in Perryton. As I stepped into the pulpit that Sunday morning I noticed a young man who looked to be about twenty-one years old. Identified as a first-time visitor, he was seated in the back pew. As the altar call was given, I saw him brush away tears from his checks. Then he stepped into the aisle and made his way to the altar where I led him in the sinner's prayer.

With the answer to my "fleece" I knew my days in Kentucky were numbered. Not yet willing to tell the people in Perryton that I would accept the position, I spent two agonizing weeks fasting and praying while trying to talk God out of the idea. But, I was unable to change His mind. My official start day as the new pastor in Perryton was the first Sunday in June.

Leaving Kentucky and the church I had attended since becoming a Christian was painful, but for Debbie, who had attended that church all of her life, it was even worse. Plus, most everyone at that church doubted our sanity. But without a doubt I knew God was sending us to Perryton. Just as God had prophesied to us through Joyce Meyer eight years earlier that we were being prepared to go to "a city that you know not of," we had never heard of Perryton and had to locate it on a roadmap.

Our first Sunday morning arrived to find us exhausted from the move and nervous wrecks concerning the future. Feeling as far from being a pastor as I was from being an astronaut, I remember standing in the hallway behind the back wall of the platform praying for the courage to even walk out. I knew I was completely unqualified to be a pastor to that wonderful group of people. Kindly introduced as their new pastors from Kentucky, I was convinced that they would soon realize our inadequacies and send us away.

After reading a scripture text I began preaching the message the Lord had laid on my heart to deliver. About fifteen minutes into my message, at a point where I had finally become comfortable, a woman raised her hand and began to motion for my attention. How unusual! Never in the thirteen years since I began preaching had anyone interrupted me during a sermon. In my insecurity, like Job I thought, "The thing that I have feared has come upon me!" Deep inside I knew she was going to say something like, "You're not a pastor," and I would have to admit it in front of all of them. My imagination was already hearing the laughter of those back in Kentucky as we returned in failure. This was going to be bad, really bad—I knew it.

Unable to ignore her any longer, I asked, "May I help you?" Her voice was so soft and kind as she asked, "Would you please pray for my mother? She's feeling very sick." I looked to the woman beside her and noted that the elderly face was deathly white.

Breathing an inward sigh of relief that my abilities were not yet in question, I walked to them, trying to look as pastoral as possible. "Let us bow our heads and pray," I said as I laid my hand on the elderly woman's right shoulder. "Heavenly Father..." I began and the unthinkable occurred when I felt her shoulder move beneath my hand. Opening my eyes at the sudden movement, I realized the woman had died! A pastor for only fifteen minutes, there I was, holding a dead lady by the shoulder!

To say I felt hopeless and helpless would be the understatement of all time. I continued to pray but so help me, I had no idea what I was saying. Watching while praying, my prayer shifted gears into begging God to do something; at the same time I was silently praying that her daughter would not open her eyes to see what had just occurred.

I sat down in the pew behind the woman, praying with all my heart while holding her by both shoulders in an attempt to keep her from falling over. Suddenly I could sense the presence of God sweep into that little church building. Like a flash of lightning, I felt something like electricity hit my hands and it stung so much that I yanked them from her and tucked them under my arms. But then my brain kicked in again and I thought, "You, nut! She's going to fall on the floor now. It's all over!"

As I reached again to grasp her shoulders, I noticed the woman was rubbing her face with both hands. God had raised her from the dead before my very eyes! I was instantly overwhelmed by the fear of the Lord. I stood quietly to my feet, bowing my head in reverence to the Lord's presence. I knew that He was right there, right then, and I had no idea what to do next. So I just stood there. It was then that I heard Him speak to my spirit something I have not forgotten to this day: "Those things you cannot do, I can do if you will look to Me."

I dismissed the service, herding the people out the door like cattle through a gate. As I shook hands, many felt the need to tell me that the woman had actually died. As if I hadn't noticed! But my desire was to get them all out of the building before someone broke the news to her, possibly creating another crisis. Finally, the last person was gone and I sat in a back pew with my face in my hands. I decided that I would not breathe a word of what had happened to anyone.

Although I never told anyone in Perryton about the miracle, immediately the church began to grow. God had confirmed my pastorate with His glorious presence. People who had never before been to church began to come to our church. In fact, I especially remember one week when we baptized thirty-one people between a Sunday morning service and the following Wednesday night. There were people coming all day long to accept Christ and be baptized.

From my experiences in Perryton I came to understand that the presence of God in one's ministry is everything. After all, we are merely an extension of His ministry. I watched Jesus in His glory build His church in Perryton. He was in control, and service after service we witnessed His glorious presence. Within a year and three months, church attendance reached 134 in a building intended to house 125.

Like Peter, James, and John, at the moment when they witnessed the transfiguration of Jesus, I knew that my life would never be the same. I could never return to life as usual. As the disciples walked off the mountain that day with Jesus, the members of His inner circle knew something about Jesus that others would only struggle to believe. They were also completely humbled by their experience on that mountaintop. Now in their hearts they knew Jesus could do anything and that He was the fulfillment of the Law and the Prophets.

The glory of God is defined in Greek and Hebrew languages as the weighted, or heavy, manifested presence of God. Unless you've had the privilege of witnessing the awesome presence of Jesus Christ operating in your earthly ministry, doing what you could never do alone, it would be hard for me to explain to you how wonderful it is, and it would be even harder for you to understand. But one thing is for certain, if you have experienced the glory of God in your ministry, you never want to attempt to do ministry alone. The only way to experience His glory is through an intimate relationship with Him.

> *THE ONLY WAY TO EXPERIENCE His GLORY IS THROUGH AN INTIMATE RELATIONSHIP WITH Him.*

Are you really ready to follow Him through the good times and the bad, regardless of where he desires to take you? If you are determined to make this journey, let me give you these climbing instructions: Focus your eyes on Jesus Christ, never let Him out of your sight, and trust Him, even when things seem impossible. With Him, all things are possible! See you on the next mountaintop.

CHAPTER 6 | MOUNTAIN OF CRUSHING

THEN, ACCOMPANIED BY THE DISCIPLES, JESUS LEFT THE
UPSTAIRS ROOM AND WENT AS USUAL TO THE MOUNT OF OLIVES.
THERE HE TOLD THEM, "PRAY THAT YOU WILL NOT BE OVERCOME BY
TEMPTATION." (LUKE 22:39–40)

As the cool evening breeze blew gently against their faces,
Jesus walked with His disciples through the Kidron Valley
toward the Mount of Olives. This short walk would lead them to
a typical setting, an olive grove. Often they had retreated here
to escape the crowd and pray. Everything seemed normal, but
shortly, their peace would be invaded with fear and uncertainty.
Though it began with a wonderful time of fellowship between
friends, it would end with a kiss of betrayal.

They had just finished eating the Passover meal together
as part of a familiar religious ceremony celebrated yearly to
commemorate the deliverance of the children of Israel from
Egyptian bondage. Passover required the death of a lamb. Each
year as a lamb was slain and its blood placed upon the doorpost
of the family home, it spoke prophetically of a new day when
the Lamb of God would come and offer Himself once and for
all to forever remove the sins of humanity. On that night as Jesus
and His disciples walked together, the prophetic fulfillment of
Passover was underway.

The Passover celebration not only centered on a lamb, but
it also included four cups, each one revealing truth concerning
the perfect Lamb of God. The first cup was known as the Cup

of Sanctification. Sanctification means "set apart for purpose." In presenting this cup, the father of the family filled a cup with wine and poured it out upon the ground as a drink offering unto God. As an act of worship, this began the Passover celebration.

As the family gathered around a table adorned in pure white, the father filled the cup with red wine a second time. Known as the Cup of Remembrance, from this cup he carefully dropped ten drops of the wine onto a white plate, and with each drop shouted out one of the ten plagues of Egypt. As he shouted, those gathered around the table chewed upon bitter herbs as a reminder of the bitterness of their Egyptian bondage. After this cup, those around the table ate their meal together.

Following the meal, the cup was filled again for a third time. Before the evening's festivities began, three loaves of unleavened bread were tucked into a napkin with three pockets. From the middle pocket, the father took the loaf, or a portion of it, wrapped it in a napkin and hid it in the house. As the third cup was filled, the father commissioned the children to search for the bread. When the retrieved bread was presented to the father, he purchased, or redeemed it back, with silver. Then he blessed the bread and wine and they were consumed together. Known as the Cup of Redemption, it is easy to see that this part of the Passover celebration is a parallel to what we in the Christian world refer to as The Lord's Supper, communion, or the sacrament.

I'll share more about the third cup later, but at this point in the ceremony the fourth cup is poured. It is a new cup, poured and set with hope before an empty place at the table. Known as Elijah's Cup, it is a symbolic reference to Malachi 4:5–6 where we find the prophecy that concludes the Old Testament. Stating that Elijah, or the spirit of Elijah, will come "to turn the hearts of the fathers to their children and the hearts of the children to their fathers," this prophecy also indicates that restoration of unity will prevent a curse on the earth.

This concluded the Passover meal but not the use of the third cup. The Cup of Redemption containing wine from the Passover meal would then be used for the following year to seal every contract, covenant, and agreement. The agreement terms would be written into a formal contract. Both parties would then cut themselves, allowing their blood to drip upon the contract. They also allowed their blood to drip into the Cup of Redemption. As they drank from the cup together, the deal was sealed and could not be broken.

Although Jesus knew the importance of the Passover meal, none of His disciples realized that their intimate dinner party was the calm before the storm. As Judas conspired with the religious leaders to betray Jesus, setting in motion the final events of God's eternal plan of redemption, Jesus felt the pressure mounting minute by minute. How did He respond?

The scripture at the beginning of this chapter tells us, "Then, accompanied by the disciples, Jesus... went as usual to the Mount of Olives." The words "as usual" speak of a pattern. Knowing the events that would unfold in the coming hours, Jesus once again retreated to a place of prayer. Upon reaching His destination on the Mount of Olives, Jesus gave His disciples a warning: "Pray that you will not be overcome by temptation." Unfortunately, the disciples did not heed His call to prayer, but rather with their bellies full of food, they catered to the flesh and nestled in for an after-dinner nap.

Jesus withdrew Himself about a stone's throw from them and fell to His knees in prayer. Caught between the divine tension of God's plan of redemption and His human desire to survive, He uttered the memorable phrase, "Father, if You are willing, take this cup from Me. Nevertheless, not My will but Thine be done" (Luke 22:42).

To what cup was Jesus referring? Quite obviously, it was the Cup of Redemption. The Father had set a price for humanity—a price that could not be changed. It would require the blood of the perfect lamb. As Jesus consented to the will of the Father in prayer, He symbolically drank from the Cup of Redemption, sealing the contract to purchase us with His own blood. By this act of submission He agreed to the torture He would experience in the coming hours, to the beating at a whipping post, and even to a cruel, shameful death on the cross. He did it all for us, knowingly and willingly, as our great High Priest.

The place where He went that night was called Gethsemane, meaning "the place of crushing." Located on the Mount of Olives, this location was nothing more than an olive press, a place where olives were crushed to produce valuable oil. A place of crushing—what a perfect place to pray! In fact, in The Living Translation of the Bible, Mark's account of the story declares that Jesus felt the crushing weight of the world on His shoulders as He said to Peter, James, and John, "My soul is crushed with grief to the point of death. Stay here and watch with Me" (Mark 14:34; NLT).

Remember that Peter, James, and John were the inner circle of Jesus' disciples who were with Him a few days earlier on another mountain when Jesus was transfigured. At that time the three witnessed Him in His glory in the presence of Moses and Elijah, but on the Mount of Olives after the Passover meal, the same three disciples looked into His grief-stricken face. The glory that had infused Jesus on the mountain where he was transfigured would be put to the test through the events that lay before Him. But Jesus would prove triumphant, coming through every test victorious as our great High Priest. The real purpose for Jesus' presence in the garden that evening after the Passover meal was to fulfill His High Priestly duties.

When God used the site of another mountain to instruct Moses to build a tabernacle, the plans He gave were patterned after the heavenly tabernacle. In that plan were three distinct sections: an outer court, an inner court, and the Holy of Holies. Only the High Priest could enter the Holy of Holies, and he could enter just once a year, when he offered a sacrifice to God for the sins of the people. Never intended to remove sin, instead those sacrifices only postponed judgment for another year.

For hundreds of years the Israelites knew what was happening behind the curtain that obscured the Holy of Holies. Every year the ritual spoke a message of hope that someday a Messiah would come and offer Himself as the eternal, acceptable sacrifice. But throughout Israel and among the disciples of Jesus, none imagined that year would be any different than the thousands before. Only God saw Jesus as the High Priest, something that even those who followed Him could not see; and God was requiring a spiritual sacrifice of this High Priest. The blood of this sacrifice would not be placed on an altar made by man, but instead would cover the mercy seat before the very throne of God in Heaven. And on that night the sacred process began outside the city walls in an olive garden, shrouded by darkness.

In December 2004, a lifetime dream came to pass for me when I visited Israel for the first time. For over thirty years I tried to imagine how the places mentioned in the Bible might look. Just stepping from the plane in Jerusalem was an overwhelming experience for me and as the days of my visit went by, it seemed there was more than my mind could contain. When I visited the place of Jesus' birth in Bethlehem, and even had the opportunity to preach there just two weeks before Christmas, it was the high point of my ministry.

When informed by our missionary that he had planned a visit to the city of Nazareth and Galilee, I could hardly wait to visit the place where Jesus had grown up and played as a young boy. Somehow, as I thought of my own childhood spent romping and playing on the hillsides of Eastern Kentucky, I connected personally with Jesus and with what He must have been like as a child.

When we finally arrived in Galilee it was much more than I could have imagined. We visited many sites in the region then made our way toward the city of Nazareth. On the way, my friend told me of a village that was set up to portray life as it was two thousand years ago and asked if I would be interested in visiting there. I agreed without hesitation, eager for a chance to see an example of life and surroundings similar to what Jesus saw and experienced when He lived on earth.

A tour of the village led us past an ancient threshing floor and a wine press. We saw how water systems were engineered to catch rainwater for drinking; then we toured terrace gardens and saw irrigation systems. It was wonderful! But the highlight came at the end of the tour as we visited an olive press. There olives from local trees hundreds of years old were pressed to produce oil that was sold to raise funds to support the re-created village. This olive press would have a profound affect on me.

The olive press was housed in a wooden shed about the size of a small barn in the United States. As a man dressed in clothing like that worn two thousand years ago explained the process, women also dressed in clothing of that period moved in and out of the shed, pouring green olives into the press from baskets they carried on their heads.

The press itself was fascinating. About five feet in diameter and cut of stone, it stood about waist high. The wall of the press was about a foot thick and I looked over the edge to see an indentation about three feet deep, big enough to hold several bushels of olives at one time. A large, round stone wheel fit tightly into the indentation and was connected to a pole to which an animal could be harnessed. As more and more olives were dumped into the press until it was completely full, the man told us that a mule pushing against the pole would make the wheel go around the indentation, grinding the olives to extract the oil.

But then something strange occurred. Although the wheel had not moved one inch, oil began to pour from the press. My curiosity made me ask the guide where all the oil was coming from. His answer was a key to revelation in my life, and I hope yours as well.

"The oil," he said, "is coming from the pressure of the other olives as they press against the ones underneath." He went on to say that what we were seeing was pure virgin olive oil, just like the oil that was used in the lamp stand in the inner court of the Tabernacle.

That statement lodged in my spirit like a seed and now, one year later, as I write this chapter, that seed has become a harvest of revelation.

Jesus was not only our great High Priest whose finished work brought an end to the need for any further sacrifice, but He, Himself, was also the olive at the olive press of Gethsemane. As He offered Himself for crushing, His blood represented our oil, for by His crushing, He gave us access to the anointing of the Holy Spirit, and that anointing destroys every yoke of bondage, bringing us to ultimate freedom.

At Gethsemane, we see the first secretion of His blood. The Bible says that Jesus' sweat became as great drops of blood. Notice that without any outward wounds being inflicted, Jesus released His first drops of blood under the pressure of you, and me, and all of humanity. Just as on the day of my visit when the virgin olive oil ran from the press due to the weight of the other olives, Jesus was crushed by the weight of the world and His blood flowed from the pores of His skin. Why? Because through submission to His Father's will, He understood the price he was to pay, the covenant was agreed upon, and He sealed the agreement by drinking from the Cup of Redemption. From that point on there was no retreat. Jesus had to go through death on the cross to finish the plan of redemption.

A study of the Old Testament reveals three stages of anointing: the leper anointing, priestly anointing, and kingly anointing. Each one of these is connected with one of the three main areas of the Tabernacle. The outer court represents the leper anointing of salvation, the inner court represents the priestly anointing of relationship, and the Holy of Holies represents the kingly anointing of authority and power.

> *A* STUDY OF THE OLD TESTAMENT REVEALS THREE STAGES OF ANOINTING: THE LEPER ANOINTING, PRIESTLY ANOINTING, AND KINGLY ANOINTING.

The Leper Anointing

The leper anointing is found in Chapter 14 of Leviticus and again in Chapter 16. When a leper was healed of his sores and the flesh-eating disease had been conquered, he was to bring two living birds and present himself to the High Priest for an anointing ritual. One of the birds was sacrificed and its blood was dripped onto the living bird. Then the living bird was sprinkled with water and released. As the bird flew away, it symbolized that blood had washed away the sin and judgment of the former leper whose life had been redeemed.

Back with Jesus at the olive press in the dark garden at Gethsemane, we can see that our High Priest secured for us that first anointing. He committed Himself to be the sacrifice that removed sin and judgment from us, allowing us to go free. His drops of blood represent our leper anointing, the salvation that could only be purchased by blood, pure blood. For centuries this anointing had been demonstrated, but in Jesus it became reality. Through Jesus, this anointing continues to be available to anyone who recognizes their need for salvation and goes to our High Priest for help.

The Priestly Anointing

The priestly anointing is the second stage and it represents our relationship with God. In Exodus 30:30, God commanded Moses to "separate Aaron and his sons as priests unto God." The first responsibility of a priest was to maintain a relationship with God. The Apostle Peter revealed to us in the New Testament that we, too, are "a chosen generation, a royal priesthood, and a holy nation that we may offer up praise to God" (1 Peter 2:9). But where would this relational anointing be secured?

The olive press holds the answer. The second pressing occurs as the stone crushes the olives. As over and over again the stone rolls around the indentation in the press, the olives are pulverized beneath it. As they are torn apart, the oil flows. Look back to the story of the events leading to the crucifixion. When we apply the example of the olive press and the second pressing, it is easier to understand what happened after Jesus was taken from the quiet garden by an angry mob and carried by Roman guards to Antonio's Fortress, also called "The Stone" or "The Pavement."

In Jesus' day, Antonio's Fortress was a place to which Roman soldiers retreated for rest and relaxation. It was in that social club for soldiers that Jesus received the most brutal beating ever known to mankind. While in Israel, I also had the privilege of visiting this unique ancient landmark. Located beneath one of Jerusalem's busy streets, the room where Jesus had been beaten was dimly lit and extremely quiet the day of my visit. Markings cut in the stone floor revealed where ancient games had been played. It was in that place where Jesus was strapped to a post and was beaten beyond recognition. What an unlikely place for such a brutal act!

I suppose to the soldiers the beating was an amusement, but to us it was much more. It was the second release of His blood, a release of even more oil, and therein, more freedom. At the moment of His beating Jesus was relating to all of us in our infirmities and weakness, and by the stripes He was receiving, we would be set free and healed.

Jesus was securing for us the priestly anointing of relationship. Through His torture, a way was being opened that we might have a relationship with God, a way that allows us to move from the outer court of salvation to an inner court of relationship and service. The beating of Jesus finally stopped, but one more stage of anointing remained.

The Kingly Anointing

The day in Nazareth when I stood beside the olive press, the guide explained the third and final stage of olive pressing. Once the wheel has pulverized the olives, extracting all the oil it can, then the stone is lifted. The mangled olive pulp is gathered and wrapped tightly in a cloth in preparation for the final extraction of olive oil. The cloth is suspended above the press and gravity itself completes the task, pulling every remaining drop of oil the olives have to give, dripping it into channels cut into the rock surface below.

My mind returns again to our High Priest as He entered the Holy of Holies with the blood of the sacrifice. The Holy of Holies represents the third anointing of kingly authority and power. Once we have walked through the outer court of salvation into the inner court of relationship, one thing yet remains—the authority and power to operate in the Kingdom.

What did the Roman soldiers do after beating Jesus? They wrapped his mangled body in a robe and in mockery placed a crown on His head. Of course, the soldiers didn't know they were preparing Jesus for His final work—the third and final shedding of His precious blood—on the cross. As gravity completed the gruesome task of pulling every drop of blood from the body of Jesus to the blood soaked ground beneath the cross, He then mustered the strength to shout one last statement: "It is finished." Upon that declaration, the veil of the temple was torn from top to bottom, and we were given access to God and the presence of the Holy Spirit through the finished work of our High Priest, Jesus Christ.

As an olive in the press, Jesus' blood secured our oil, a precious anointing that broke the bondage of our sin, our loneliness, and our hopelessness and in turn, gave us salvation, a relationship with God, and an opportunity to reign with Him in His eternal Kingdom. Our anointing for ministry—past, present and future—is forever directly related to the finished work of our High Priest, Jesus Christ.

The psalmist of Psalm 133 describes it best as he paints a picture using the anointing of Aaron as the high priest. He shares how the oil flows from the head, all the way down to the skirt and the hem of his garment. Jesus is the true High Priest. It is His anointing that flows down over the body as we come into submission to His lordship as the Head of the Church. In fact, because the greatest amount of oil was at the hem of the garment, the principle we learn as we look at this example is that the lower we humble ourselves, the greater the level of anointing. As we bow at His feet, we can expect the anointing of God to increase in our life.

All of us are going to experience crushing blows in our lives and our ministry, but instead of allowing those experiences to drive us away from God, we should learn from Jesus in the Garden of Gethsemane and allow those pressures to drive us to our knees.

My Olive Press Years

Over my years of traveling, I've had the opportunity to visit in the homes of literally hundreds of pastors. Inevitably, the conversation turns to a particular period in their life and ministry when they didn't know whether or not they would survive. I've come to call those times the crushing years. If we are truly followers of Jesus Christ, there is an olive press awaiting us all.

My olive press time spanned a three-year period beginning in 1989. After two successful years pastoring in Perryton, Texas, we had become somewhat accustomed to seeing the glory of God being poured out service after service. Each week people were giving their lives to Jesus and things were going very well, at least that was my opinion. Once the church building was filled to capacity, I approached the church board that had, up to that point, been extremely supportive. But when I suggested expanding the facilities to accommodate the growing crowds, there was immediate opposition. I was told that the church had been built by a very wealthy man under an agreement that the building never be altered in any way. The news was baffling— how could anyone feel more love for bricks and mortar than for living human beings?

Even more bizarre was the news that the man's family held the deed to the church. How could a family own a church, I questioned. Feeling certain that couldn't be true, I investigated. Public records revealed that not only was it true, but that the family's consent would be needed for any type of expansion.

My investigation into the matter did not lead to a peaceful solution but instead to my eviction from the property. I had personally done nothing to warrant an attack, but in the opinion of those in control the church had grown too large under my leadership. I found myself unemployed, homeless, and with a large number of new converts who were looking to me for answers to the situation. Metaphorically, I could feel myself sweating blood. What was I supposed to do? What about my family's needs? What about the new converts who were just newborn lambs—could they survive without a shepherd?

My phone rang continually with calls from people who loved us and who wanted to know why we were leaving them when things were going so well. I had tried to peacefully resign the church in secret but that secret could not be kept. The more I wrestled with the situation, the more I realized I couldn't leave the baby Christians to fend for themselves, for I knew that as their shepherd, I would stand before God responsible for each of them. As far as they were concerned, nothing had changed; they were oblivious to the newfound discoveries with which I was dealing.

The decision I made is one I have struggled with for years—was it right or wrong? I still don't know; some questions only eternity will answer. I started a new church. Named Emmanuel Fellowship, the church was founded on one desire—to mature the "little lambs" God had placed in my care.

To paraphrase Charles Dickens in the opening of his book *A Tale of Two Cities*, the next two years were the best of times and the worst of times. While I was thrilled at the progression of those young lambs into mature Christians, our family's financial stability was being undermined as I personally took on financial obligations that should have been carried by the church. Then a recession hit our little town in the form of an oil crisis, and the major oil companies providing employment for many members of our church began relocating elsewhere. In order to keep their employment, many families were forced to move; others in the church found themselves unemployed. As for me, I was drowning in credit card debt, just trying to survive.

By 1991, it became evident that the church was not going to survive. Figuratively, in my own "press," I was also bleeding heavily under the crushing weight of the moment. I found myself asking God over and over, "What should I do?"

Then one day while I prayed, the answer came. During our

transition to forming a new church, two pastors in town had been especially supportive of our venture, even offering to pay the rent for the church building if I remained in town. Although I didn't accept their offer because they, too, were feeling the pinch of the recession, the two pastors had become like brothers to me. I called them both and scheduled a meeting.

When we met, I told them that I believed I had a God-inspired idea. My suggestion was that we set our own personal ministry ambitions aside and merge the churches together into one strong church that could survive the oil crunch. We agreed to pray the idea through. After several meetings to talk discuss the logistics of such a merger, we came to agreement that this was indeed the direction of God. Fifteen years later as I look back, God's direction for the merger is evident because that church has flourished, is still going strong, and is now located in a new, larger facility.

But merging three churches into one does not require three pastors. Once again I found myself unemployed, and this time $20,000 in debt as well. As we prepared to leave Texas and return to Kentucky, I was completely unaware that a final crushing was awaiting me.

We moved in with my in-laws, convinced that it was a temporary arrangement that would last a few weeks until we could get on our feet. But weeks turned into months. There were no invitations to preach anywhere and no pastoral opportunities in sight. For a year I found myself pressed until every drop of hope was gone from my mind. During that period I actually prayed asking God to just take me home if He was through with me here on earth.

Eventually I came to understand that during that time God was more interested in doing something in me than He was in doing something through me. Apparently I needed a final crushing, and no one knew it better than He. It was during that time of being in the "press" that a new level of anointing was released that would enable me to carry out the mission that was yet to come. Like the olives, every crushing blow we receive releases new anointing oil that enables us to carry out His will. Not only do we need His glory to confirm us as we discovered in the last chapter, but we also need the power of the Holy Spirit to help us walk out the journey step by step.

> *EVENTUALLY I CAME TO UNDERSTAND THAT DURING THAT TIME GOD WAS MORE INTERESTED IN DOING SOMETHING IN ME THAN HE WAS IN DOING SOMETHING THROUGH ME.*

Oftentimes we find ourselves in a situation resembling the story of Mary as recounted in Matthew 26 and the gospels of Mark and Luke as well. Our ministry is an alabaster box that we have worked so hard to fill with treasures. We want it to look pretty but to keep everything hidden inside. But no one knows what we are really like until we ourselves are broken. It is then that the fragrance of His presence fills the room, and we come to the realization that God is indeed faithful and true and that we can trust Him in the good times and the bad.

So, as we leave the mountain of crushing and stumble our way toward the next mountaintop, let us never forget that His grace is sufficient for what lies ahead. Hold firmly to the promise that He will never leave us nor forsake us, and realize that His strength is made perfect in our weakness. So look up and no matter how steep the mountain, keep climbing, for this is certainly no place to stop. There is victory ahead!

CHAPTER 7 | MOUNTAIN OF ULTIMATE SACRIFICE

AND HE BEARING HIS CROSS WENT FORTH INTO A PLACE CALLED THE PLACE OF A SKULL, WHICH IS CALLED IN THE HEBREW GOLGOTHA. (JOHN 19:17)

Although the crucifixion of Jesus is depicted in all four Gospels, the simple yet profound description in the gospel of John uniquely captures the loneliness Jesus felt at that time. Throughout His ministry, Jesus had been thronged by multitudes of needy people. But at the crucifixion, His greatest time of need, Jesus had to face it alone. The multitude had abandoned Him; those who had shouted "Hosanna" were now shouting "Crucify!" The seventy disciples had fled in fear, ten of the twelve disciples were in hiding, and two of Jesus' three closest disciples were running for their lives.

Jesus found Himself facing the cruelest death imaginable with only one disciple and His mother at His side, and they were clueless as to why His life must end that way. Questions must have flooded over them. What about the new Kingdom He said would come? What about the victory He promised to those who would follow Him? And how could He lead a revolt against Roman tyranny while hanging on a cross?

As confusion intensified, Mary found herself in a position no mother should have to face—witnessing the public execution of her son, knowing full well that He was innocent of all charges against Him. No doubt she rehearsed every precious moment they had experienced together: His birth and bed in a stable manger in Bethlehem; His first trip to the temple and Simon's confirmation that his eyes had seen the Messiah; Jesus as a little boy; Jesus at twelve when they had lost Him among the shuffle and later found Him in the temple confounding the scholars; and at her bidding, Jesus performing His first miracle at the wedding in Cana of Galilee. In a grief that could not comprehend, Mary must have walked step by step through the corridors of her memory, wondering why this thirty-three-year journey would end on a cross with Jesus treated as a common criminal.

Most Bible scholars agree that Joseph had died before Jesus was crucified. Loss of the head of the household would leave Jesus, as the eldest son, responsible for the well-being of Mary and His family. But Mary found herself alone and confused by the events of the previous twenty-four hours. Questions must have raced through her mind. "Is this it?" "Is it over?" "What about the men who follow Jesus? What will they do now? Will they, too, face martyrs' deaths?" Deep in her heart Mary knew Jesus was God and that He had the power to do something. Every fiber of her body must have been crying out for Him to save Himself. But Mary also was completely unaware that Jesus was paying the price that would save all humanity.

> *As FOLLOWERS OF JESUS, EACH OF US HAS A CROSS WAITING.*

As followers of Jesus, each of us has a cross waiting. In fact, Jesus Himself tells us to take up our cross and follow Him. While it is true that our cross may not be a wooden one like the cross of Jesus, but there will come a time of ultimate sacrifice. At that time, as you feel the sting of loneliness, you will become fully aware that the only option available is to completely obey your Heavenly Father's direction. At such a time, friends may forsake you and colleagues won't understand. Possibly even your family and those to whom you are closest may doubt your sanity as your allegiance and commitment to God are put to the ultimate test.

After the struggles my family experienced in Texas, and after a year of unemployment, I grew accustomed to sitting on my in-laws' porch day after day, wondering if my best days were behind me. But the tide began to change with the birth of the new year of 1992.

As a family we began attending Christian Fellowship Church in the autumn of 1991. Through our connection with Dr. J. T. Parish, we received our first ray of light, bringing an end to a very dark season. Dr. Parish alone had reached out to me from Kentucky when I pastored in Texas. In my difficult times, he often sent what I called care packages that contained tapes, books, or other materials. He also was an invaluable help during the incorporation process for the new church we started. In fact, he had been a true father to me in every way, without any ulterior motives on his part. He had been a father because he was a father.

I remember that the first night I visited Christian Fellowship Church with my family, Dr. Parish came to us and asked, "How can we help you?" How refreshing! Every other church we visited greeted us with a reverse of that statement that went something like this: "You can sure help us if you decide to make this your home church." We realized that we needed healing so Debbie and I decided to make Christian Fellowship

Church our home.

After a few months, Dr. Parish connected us with a church in Providence, Kentucky, that was looking for a pastor. Because the leaders of that church respected Dr. Parish greatly, they invited us, sight unseen, upon his recommendation. I was to serve as interim pastor until they could find a permanent pastor to fill the pulpit. We were overjoyed at the new venture. It was so great to be preaching again after being out of work for so long.

The Providence church was awesome! The church facility was new and gorgeous, with plenty of room for growth; plus, the financial condition of the church was good. The congregation was mostly young, many were near our age, and best of all, the members loved and accepted us. And boy did we need their love by that time! Founded by a pastor who served the congregation until just before our arrival, the church members were still mourning his departure to a new field of service. Of course, we were mourning too, but for different reasons. So God, in His wisdom, used that time for our mutual healing. We needed them; they needed us. It was a perfect match.

On top of all of that, the Board of Directors informed me that they would be paying me $700 per week as interim pastor— double any weekly wage I had earned to that point! Daring to hope again, I thought perhaps with that income we could chip away at the debt we had accumulated just trying to survive. I couldn't have painted a better scenario for myself and I was so grateful to God.

Because we were still living with my in-laws, two or three times each week I made the two hundred-mile round trip to

Providence. I was delighted to do it, and the drive provided an ideal time for me to pray and seek God's master plan for my life and for the future of that wonderful church. Often I visited families connected with the church and as I drove through street after street, I found myself praying, believing God to impact that little community.

The church began to grow, doubling in size in only three months. Many who had been discouraged by the departure of their greatly loved pastor turned and encircled the Clendenen family in welcome. Once again, we felt the presence of God greeting us service after service, bringing healing to all. There was such a sense of love and unity, a bond that strengthened every time we came together. I was so happy to finally be pastoring again, believed I was serving the greatest church in the whole world, and thought it couldn't get any better.

The previous few years had been hard on my family. As is often the case, when you're going through the olive press you lose sight of its effect on those who love you the most. Self-consumed in my own pain, I confess my guilt in that regard. Our difficulties had not only affected my life and that of my immediate family, but it had also affected my mother and my siblings. Still living in the small rural town where I was raised, they were constantly asked how I was doing. What could they say? They didn't want to admit the embarrassing truth that I was living with my in-laws and hadn't preached in some time. But with our pastoral service at Providence, that was behind us. My family could again feel a sense of pride that I was back, pastoring a great church. Some of my family even came to visit that church with us.

One day while I was traveling alone and praying, my heart became very troubled. Although I knew God wanted to tell me something, I wasn't sure what, so I set aside some time to be alone with Him. During that time alone with Him, I felt a deep sense of appreciation swell within me. Wave after wave of gratitude and thanksgiving flooded my spirit and I began to rehearse the faithfulness of God, thanking Him for Dr. J. T. Parish. After all, I knew it was Dr. Parish's influence that had made our transition to the Providence church possible.

Like the mother of Jesus, my mind began to retrace the steps that had brought me to that place. I thought of how Dr. Parish had counseled me during the difficult moments at People's Chapel in Perryton, Texas. When I left People's Chapel, he had gone to great lengths to help me structure Emmanuel Fellowship in that community. I thought of the many times Dr. Parish had sent books and tapes, and of all he had done to support us during the most difficult years of our lives and ministry. That day, alone with God, I thanked God not only for Dr. Parish, but for Christian Fellowship Church as well, for it was their love and kindness that had also helped us regain our footing.

As my private worship service continued and tears streamed down my face, I heard the Holy Spirit speak softly to me, saying, "Now is the time for you to serve Dr. Parish and Christian Fellowship like they have served you and your family."

Unable to process what that might mean, I didn't dare breathe what I had heard to anyone, and like Mary, just pondered those things in my heart. I didn't even tell Debbie because I thought I'd have plenty of time to do that later. That afternoon as I prepared to work on the message I would preach at Providence the following Sunday I wondered what I was going to say to the church about the Holy Spirit's instructions. Another question followed: How in the world would I approach Dr. Parish?

Sunday morning came and we made our way toward Providence. I knew somehow that God would make it happen in His own time. Although in the dark on the how and the when, I knew one thing for sure—my assignment that morning was to preach and I tried to keep that as my focus. The church was packed, everyone seemed unusually happy, and the service began with a wonderful time of worship. Later I discovered that the pastor search committee and congregation had been meeting privately and had decided that Sunday was the day to inform me that their search for a new pastor was over. But in their excitement they had forgotten to fill me in!

Suddenly, the elder in charge of the service shouted, "How would you like to have the Clendenens as our new pastors?" The people responded with applause and a standing ovation; instantly I felt the tension of the moment. God had spoken to me privately on Thursday, and now the people were voting publicly in a Sunday morning service. Before I could collect my thoughts, the elder motioned me to the platform. I suppose everyone was expecting my acceptance speech.

Standing at the pulpit, I began to weep. My heart was overwhelmed with emotion and I could feel their love and support. I began by telling them how much I loved them and that we were honored that they would even consider us to be their pastors. Going on, I told them that nothing would please me more, but that unfortunately God had spoken to me on Thursday to go a different direction. Believing they needed to know why I was declining their offer, I went on to explain that God was calling us to serve Dr. Parish and Christian Fellowship Church. Their smiles faded but they graciously received the news. Swallowing hard, I preached my message, and concluded the service by telling them my exit date. The service ended on a positive note as we hugged one another and thanked God for our time together. After embracing the last couple, we made our way to the car for a long, quiet drive home.

Debbie, always practical while I am impulsive, finally broke the silence. "Don't you think you should tell Dr. Parish your plan," she asked, "since you've just announced it to three hundred people?" Brilliant idea! As soon as we reached home, I called Dr. Parish and set an appointment for the next morning.

When I arrived at Christian Fellowship Church, I felt like a soldier reporting for duty although I had never been drafted. Dr. Parish, a precious man who had been such a great help to us, greeted me with his typical tenderness and asked, "Brother Rick, how are things going in Providence?"

I smiled and told him things were great, then added there was something else I wanted to talk about. "The real reason I called for this appointment," I told him, "is that I believe that God is calling me to make Christian Fellowship Church my home, and I would like to serve here if I can."

He smiled and I continued, "After all, I announced to the church yesterday that I was going to come here and serve you. Is that possible?"

Concerned for the well being of our family, he told me that at that time the church was not able to afford an additional staff member. And he said that they probably wouldn't be able to pay us even a third of what we were making there at Providence. I assured him the pay didn't matter—I just wanted to obey God and to keep my word with the congregation in Providence. God was in charge of everything else, I told him.

I'm sure that must have been the strangest interview Dr. Parish has ever conducted, especially since he hadn't set out to hire anyone that day. But he agreed to let us come and serve him and the church. We never discussed responsibilities or titles, or any of the normal things usually discussed at such times. As for me, I was thrilled that the words I had spoken to the church members in Providence actually became reality. As unusual as it was, that meeting set the stage for the rest of my life.

For the next six years I served the church in a variety of ways, doing whatever needed to be done. Dr. Parish had a radio program and to take a burden from him, I began producing the programs. I worked as Minister of Ministry Development, establishing a ministry of helps with greeters, ushers, altar workers, and others. My focus was to build the infrastructure to make the church stronger. The results of my efforts were behind the scenes, out of the limelight. But aside from occasionally teaching classes, I was not in pulpit ministry. God had assured me that if I could be faithful with that which belonged to another, He would give me my own ministry.

Debbie and I were never more content. She eventually joined the church staff as a secretary and God blessed our efforts as we supported our pastors. We witnessed an increase in our anointing and also saw the blessings of the Lord being poured over our lives. Our children attended Christian Fellowship School and as a family we all grew stronger in every way. We were all very content.

Even though everything was going great for us, my ministry friends and even my family had many questions. Well meaning people who loved us dearly often asked why we were out of pastoral ministry. There were questions concerning why we were serving in a church that already had seven staff members. "You're bigger than this," we often heard. "You can pastor your own church."

Somehow, for many people, the concept of success does not include serving others, but rather, being served by others. For my mother and siblings, one of their biggest concerns was over our finances. They knew the sacrifices we had made in Texas and they also knew our present financial status. Therefore, the decision to serve as we were serving at Christian Fellowship made no sense to them and had the appearance of a demotion rather than a promotion. But I knew deep in my heart that God was in control. The choices before me were simple—to obey or disobey His direction in my life. Sometimes we must look to God to defend us, especially when our words ring hollow in the ears of those who are looking for answers but who have already drawn their own conclusions.

> GOD HAS NOT CALLED US TO DEFEND EVERY ACTION WE TAKE, BUT RATHER TO BE OBEDIENT TO HIS PERFECT WILL.

God has not called us to defend every action we take, but rather to be obedient to His perfect will. If we obey Him and submit completely to His will, we can rest assured that He will prove us in due season.

As Jesus hung on the cross, He knew what it was to be misunderstood and lonely. Those who loved Him most were not convinced He had made right choices. All along they misunderstood what it would take to accomplish His plan, not understanding that the cross was indeed the plan of God. But to Jesus, opinions didn't matter. The feelings of others could not change Him, and the criticisms of observers could not prevent Him from accomplishing His mission. He knew that His mission was greater than their perspective or even their ability to comprehend. Jesus identified with the needs of humanity. His actions that day changed the course of history and opened the door to eternity.

With our human limitations, it is easy to look back and recognize that no one but Jesus could grasp the significance of that one moment in time. Never before, or since, was there a day so revolutionary. Heaven, Earth and Hell all stood at attention, focused on one little hillside while Jesus, our High Priest, carried out God's perfect plan of redemption.

For six hours, the living drama unfolded as Jesus hung suspended between Heaven and Earth as the sacrificial Lamb of God. During those grueling hours, He uttered just seven statements, but with each statement, He directly identified with seven needs that we all face in life. He was identifying with those who could not identify with Him.

"Father, forgive them for they know not what they do."

History tells us that Jesus' spoke his first statement around nine o'clock in the morning as the angry mob mocked and jeered Him. Although those in the crowd were unaware of their own need of forgiveness, Jesus realized their need and knew that only He could purchase forgiveness through His death, burial, and resurrection. Once again, as was His custom, Jesus retreated to prayer. But He did not pray for Himself, or even for strength to endure the moment. Instead, He stood in the High Priestly role of intercession, taking our need for forgiveness before the Father. He prayed, "Father forgive them, for they know not what they do" (Luke 23:34). Thanks be to God that things have never changed! Jesus is still our great intercessor, ever living to make intercession for us.

"Today, shalt thou be with Me in Paradise."

After nearly two more hours of suffering in silence, the two criminals being crucified with Jesus began to talk to Him. One of them joined with the crowd in mockery, but the other came to realize that Jesus was truly the Son of God. In desperation, he asked Jesus to remember him. Jesus responded with a statement of hope, "Today, shalt thou be with Me in Paradise" (Luke 23:43). That message of hope rings throughout generations and we know that even now, to be absent from the body is to be present with the Lord. And, according to Colossians 1:27, "Christ in you, the hope of glory."

"Woman, behold thy son." Then saith He to the disciple, "Behold thy mother."

This statement, as recorded in John 19:26–27, was spoken on the heels of Jesus' prayer. Moved with compassion for those He would leave behind, especially for His mother, His concern at that moment was not for their Heavenly security, but rather their earthly security. His death would also provide for us here on earth. As a loving son, He focused on securing the needs of His mother, but as a loving Savior, He was also securing the needs of all believers who put their faith in Him. What He purchased that day is still in effect. Philippians 4:19 declares: "My God shall supply all your need according to His riches in glory by Christ Jesus."

"My God, My God, why hast Thou forsaken Me?"

The historical account reveals that Jesus made this statement nearly two and one-half hours after He spoke to His mother and John, the longest time of silence from the cross. In the meantime, the sun refused to shine and darkness covered the land creating, literally, the darkest moment in the history of the world as Jesus, alone, bore the sins of mankind. God the Father was forced to turn away from His only Son.

From that place of abandonment, Jesus cried out, "My God, My God, why hast Thou forsaken Me?" (Matthew 27:46). In that cry, He was identifying with all humanity and the sin that separated them from a relationship with a holy God. Never again would anyone have to feel rejection and abandonment. Because of Jesus' obedience, there would be a new and living way established, securing forever our relationship with God. In Hebrews 13:5, we can still find these comforting words, "I will never leave thee, nor forsake thee."

"I thirst."

By the time Jesus uttered these words He had been hanging on the cross for more than five hours with His body wracked with pain. We see His humanity surfacing with just two words: "I thirst" (John 19:28). One hundred percent human, Jesus was totally man in every way, even though He remained without sin. But in moments like this on the cross, Jesus identified with our weakness and our pain. As High Priest, He is touched by the feelings of our infirmities. Although He died a thirsty man, through His sacrificial death our need for natural and spiritual water was paid in full and we would never have to thirst again. His obedience purchased rivers of living water for us and validated the invitation given in John 7:37–38: "In the last day, that great [day] of the feast, Jesus stood and cried, saying, "'If any man thirst, let him come unto me, and drink. He that believeth on me, as the scripture hath said, out of his belly shall flow rivers of living water."'

"It is finished."

The final two statements made by Jesus on the cross were spoken in succession as the time neared three o'clock in the afternoon, the designated time when Passover lambs were to be slaughtered in order to postpone judgment for another year. But that year, the Lamb of God laid down His life once and for all, removing the guilt of sin forever. "It is finished" (John 19:30) referred to the completion of God's plan of redemption. Man's sin brought about death and required a sacrifice—not just any sacrifice, but the sacrifice of a perfect man. Adam had been created in a perfect state, but as the result of his sin the entire human race was in need of redemption. Only a sinless sacrifice, a perfect man, could redeem man to his previous relationship with God. Jesus met all the requirements the law demanded; those three simple words signaled man's reconciliation back to God. Romans 5:19 says it best: "For as by one man's disobedience many were made sinners, so by the obedience of one shall many be made righteous."

"Father, into Thy hands I commend My spirit."

The final words of Jesus, as recorded in Luke 23:46, were spoken at three o'clock in the afternoon, and then He died. These words spoke of rest. The work was accomplished, the price was paid, and eternal peace and rest were available to all who put their trust in Him. That rest and peace are still available as substantiated by Hebrews 4:9: "There remaineth therefore a rest to the people of God."

In order to enter that rest, the scripture goes on to declare that we must cease from our own works and trust in His finished work. This peace and rest cannot be earned by human effort or by our own works of self-righteousness. We must learn that it comes by grace and by putting our faith in the Lord Jesus Christ.

Seven is the number of completion. With these seven statements, Jesus completed the plan of redemption, even though none of the onlookers that day understood the full scope of what was happening. Some were mocking, others were weeping, but all would be given an equal opportunity to receive the blessings connected with His obedience.

The same holds true in our lives today. Never does our obedience to God affect only the life of the individual, for none of us is an island unto ourselves. Our actions have a domino effect on the lives of those connected to us. Our times of ultimate sacrifice can open doors to seasons of blessing for others. Disobedience to God has repercussions as well. We can be a stumbling block or an open door; the choice is ours. That is why it is so important that we not shy away from our responsibilities as believers.

Each of us needs to pick up the cross we have been given and obediently follow Him, even through lonely times when we are misunderstood or even mocked. But as each of us follows in obedience, we must remember to hold firm, knowing that the mountain of ultimate sacrifice is not the end, but instead is just another step of the journey leading to ultimate victory ahead. Don't stop climbing; the best is yet to come.

CHAPTER 8 | MOUNTAIN OF HOPE

The apostles were at the Mount of Olives when this happened, so they walked the half mile back to Jerusalem.

(Acts 1:12; NLT)

Reading this scripture out of context one may question to what the words "when this happened" referred. It was the ascension of Jesus Christ from Earth into Heaven. Because of what happened, the place where this occurred is often referred to as the Mountain of Ascension, but, in fact, the location was the top of the Mount of Olives. During my visit to Jerusalem I had a perfect view of that historic site from the window in my room at the Seven Arches Hotel. Every night I struggled to pull myself away from the window as my eyes kept being drawn to where Jesus had lifted into the Heavens. I wondered what the disciples must have thought as they were first-hand witnesses to the event.

For the followers of Jesus, the month and a half before had been a whirlwind. In the first three days alone they witnessed His arrest, heard the false accusations, saw Him beaten and crucified, and then saw Him raised from the dead. The forty days after that were equally difficult to fathom. Jesus suddenly appeared inside locked rooms, they ate with Him, and at His encouragement touched His body. They knew He was more than a spirit, but they certainly didn't understand the new glorified body He possessed. Each day must have been a new adventure as Jesus reminded them of all the lessons He taught them before the crucifixion, powerful lessons that molded and shaped their lives.

On the day of His ascension, the disciples surrounded Jesus, hanging on His every word as they climbed the Mount of Olives for what would be their eighth and final mountaintop experience with Him. Eight is the number of new beginnings and they certainly had a new beginning in store.

Everyone could sense it was an important time. Preparing them with last-minute instructions, Jesus said, "Don't leave Jerusalem until you receive the gift of the Holy Spirit" (Acts 1:4; paraphrased). Then He went on to say, "Ye shall receive power after the Holy Spirit is come upon you. You shall be witnesses unto Me both in Jerusalem, and in all Judea, and in all Samaria, and unto the uttermost parts of the earth" (Acts 1:8).

Luke describes what happened next in the simplest of words: "While he was blessing them, he left them and was taken up to heaven" (Luke 24:51; NLT).

Put yourself in the disciples' sandals and imagine what they must have experienced as they strained for a last glimpse of Jesus as He vanished into the clouds. In complete wonder and amazement, each must have been afraid to even move. But suddenly, the silence was broken when two angels appeared and said, "Men of Galilee, why are you standing here staring at the sky? Jesus has been taken away from you into Heaven. And someday, just as you saw Him go, He will return" (Acts 1:11; paraphrased).

What a powerful promise of hope! Before they even had time to process His going, they were given a dynamic promise of His return. Like the water of a spring, lesson after lesson Jesus had taught them bubbled to the surface as they traced the steps that had brought them to that place of departure. They remembered what He had told them in the Upper Room when He announced He would be leaving them. They had become distraught as He uttered the words of encouragement found in John 14:1–3: "Let not your heart be troubled: ye believe in God, believe also in me. In my Father's house are many mansions: if it were not so, I would have told you. I go to prepare a place for you. And if I go and prepare a place for you, I will come again, and receive you unto Myself; that where I am, there ye may be also."

At that point I have no doubt that they began to share promise after promise Jesus had made to them. Someone must have said, "Do you remember what He said when we were gathered with Him in the Upper Room? 'Nevertheless, I tell you, it is expedient for you that I go away. For if I go not away, the Comforter will not come unto you. But if I depart, I will send Him to you'" (John 16:7).

I can almost hear another disciple saying, "He also told us that when the Spirit of Truth is come, He will guide us into all truth. For He will not speak of Himself, for whatsoever He hears that will He speak and He will show us things to come" (John 16:13).

As they walked the half mile distance toward Jerusalem, hope was rising in their hearts, making a place for their faith to reside. Hebrews 11:1 tells us: "Now faith is the substance of things hoped for, the evidence of things not seen." The disciples were walking back to Jerusalem without Jesus but not without hope, for He had promised that He, Himself, would come again. Until the day of His return, the Holy Spirit He promised to send would guide them (and us) throughout our various journeys. For the disciples, the time had come to believe and obey His instructions. One hundred-twenty strong, they gathered in a room, awaiting the outpouring of the Holy Spirit.

With the angelic declaration following Jesus' ascension to Heaven, hope was born for all who put their faith in the Lord Jesus Christ and who hold on to the promises He made us—hope for eternity and hope for tomorrow. We know that someday He will return and we will rule and reign with Him throughout eternity. We also know that the Holy Spirit has come to dwell in us right now, in this life; His presence enables us to carry out the Great Commission Jesus assigned to His followers.

I refer to the eternity and tomorrow dimensions of hope as long-range and short-range hope. Our long-range hope of Heaven is attained the instant we accept Jesus Christ and His finished work. Romans 10:9–10 declares that as we confess with our mouth the Lord Jesus and believe in our heart that God has raised Him from the dead, we can be certain that our hope of eternity in Heaven with Him is secured. Christ in us is our hope of glory, and that hope is an anchor for the soul that is sure and steadfast.

The second dimension of hope is short-range hope. Not instantly attained, instead this hope comes through a deliberate process. Later in the New Testament, the Apostle Paul described both dimensions of hope and explained in detail the process by which short-range hope is developed: "Therefore being justified by faith, we have peace with God through our Lord Jesus Christ: By whom also we have access by faith into this grace wherein we stand, and rejoice in hope of the glory of God. And not only [so], but we glory in tribulations also: knowing that tribulation worketh patience; And patience, experience; and experience, hope: And hope maketh not ashamed; because the love of God is shed abroad in our hearts by the Holy Ghost which is given unto us" (Romans 5:1–5).

Notice that the fifth chapter of Romans begins with verses 1 and 2 clearly explaining the long-range hope that accompanies our justification by faith. It is called our hope of the glory of God. Verses 3 through 5 begin to reveal the step-by-step process by which our short-range hope is developed.

Step One: We Glory in Tribulation

The difficulties in the step-by-step process begin right away with the statement that we are to "glory in tribulation." I've not quite mastered Step One. My natural response to tribulation can be categorized as more grumbling than glory. But, the same exhortation is reiterated in James 1:2: "My brethren, count it all joy when ye fall into divers temptations..."

In both cases, the instruction is focused on our attitude. None of us can control the circumstances of life, or the situations that confront us day by day. But all of us have the ability to control what happens in us. That's where our attitude comes into the picture. Our attitude determines our altitude in the sense that God will not promote us past the level of our attitude.

Realize that God uses the process to build our character and no one knows better how to do it than God. We can rest in the knowledge that nothing ever touches our life that has not been sifted through His fingers, and that all things will work together for our good (Romans 8:28).

> *OUR ATTITUDE DETERMINES OUR ALTITUDE IN THE SENSE THAT GOD WILL NOT PROMOTE US PAST THE LEVEL OF OUR ATTITUDE.*

Step Two: Tribulation Works Patience

How ironic! The very tribulation that tries my patience also develops it at the same time. Patience is a virtue birthed of difficulty. Early in my Christian walk I learned not to pray for patience; doing so was like putting out a welcome mat for trouble. But at this juncture in my life, I have come to appreciate the value of the struggles I've had to endure. Those struggles have produced the inward strength and resolve necessary for endurance. I have found Him to be faithful and true; His hand will truly never guide me where His grace cannot sustain me. His light shines brightest in the darkest moments. Don't despair, grasp the promise found in James 1:4: "But let patience have her perfect work, that ye may be perfect and entire, wanting nothing."

Step Three: Patience Brings Experience

Tribulation cannot be conquered without patience. Through patience we win the battle over every struggle life has to offer. The truth of the matter is that Christians cannot lose unless they quit! As we learn to hold on to God and His promises, He proves Himself faithful and our test becomes our testimony. As each experience builds on the last, an undisputable track record of victory is formed, becoming a testimony that is part of the arsenal by which we defeat the enemy. Revelation 12:11 declares: "And they overcame him by the blood of the Lamb, and by the word of their testimony; and they loved not their lives unto the death." Each individual's testimony is different because our lives are different. There is no such thing as a good testimony or a bad one. But each personal testimony carries the power to defeat the enemy.

Step Four: Experience Brings Hope

With every experience, the thought of eternity becomes

sweeter and the challenges of tomorrow more possible. Short-range hope develops as we witness His faithfulness day after day through the battles of life. We can look back and realize that He has been faithful, and we look forward with the hope that He will never leave us nor forsake us. The greatest evidence that He will be faithful tomorrow is found in the fact that He was faithful yesterday. You can trust Him for your eternity and you can trust Him for the struggle you face today. Hebrews 13:8 (NLT) declares that "Jesus Christ is the same yesterday, today, and forever." Be assured that God is at work, establishing a victorious testimony in your life.

Testimony played a vital role in the everyday lives of God's people during biblical times. As the children of Israel moved from Egypt to their promised land, God instructed them to set up memorials at various places where He supernaturally met their needs. Those memorials stood as a visible testimony of the faithfulness of God even to future generations.

In Bible times, shepherds had a unique way of displaying their testimony. As part of the passage to manhood, each young shepherd was given his own staff. He used that staff not only to shepherd sheep, but also to chronicle the victories of his life. It became a symbol of his testimony carried in his hand.

Beginning at the bottom of the staff, the shepherd made carvings to remind him of pivotal moments in his life. Shepherds are by nature nomadic, moving from place to place in search of pasture land. For amusement, they passed the time at night telling stories around the fire. Their staffs became a central point for their conversations. Pointing to a particular carving on another's staff, the staff's owner would be asked to tell the story to which it related. Over and over the shepherds rehearsed their struggles and victories. Although always traveling and with surroundings always changing, one's testimony remained consistent as a stabilizing force in a nomadic life. Not only did it provide fodder for storytelling, but it also served much more meaningful purposes. Two of these purposes are substantiated in scripture.

Our Testimony Prepares Us for Our Present Battle

In 1 Samuel 17 is found the story of a shepherd boy named David, sent by his father to a battlefield to deliver cheese to his brothers, a trip that would result in him delivering Israel from her Philistine enemies. When David arrived at the Israelite camp, all the soldiers were gripped with fear over a giant who screamed for someone to defend Israel and their God's integrity. The odds were overwhelmingly against anyone defeating the giant who had been a warrior from his youth. Although every soldier was armed with weaponry, David had only a shepherd's staff in his hand. But that staff was a critical part of the weaponry he used to defeat the giant Philistine. As David volunteered to fight the enemy champion, the warriors of Israel mocked and scorned him, even though none of them were willing to fight. Finally, David was sent to King Saul.

At first, Saul chuckled at the thought of the young shepherd boy going against a champion like Goliath, but he had no other option. So he tried to equip David with his own armor but Saul's armor didn't fit the young man. Then David, with a shepherd's staff in his hand, pointed to the carvings and began to tell the king of Israel a story.

"Once I was keeping my father's sheep," he began. "Do you see this mark on the bottom of my staff? This was the first victory God gave me. When a lion came to attack and destroy the sheep I was commissioned to protect, the Spirit of the Lord came upon me, enabling me to destroy him. But that's not all! You see the second mark here, just above the first? Again, I was alone, protecting the sheep, when a bear came out of the woods. The bear seemed a lot larger than the lion but the same Spirit of the Lord came upon me again, and I was able to kill the bear and deliver the sheep from his clutches. Now I stand here before you with a new enemy that is larger than any I've faced before. But greater is He that is within me than the giant standing before me."

In I Samuel 17:40, the first weapon mentioned in David's arsenal was the staff in his hand. Why would a shepherd take his staff into battle? The answer is that he was expecting soon to carve out a new victory. There was no doubt in David's mind that the faithful God of yesterday would also be the victorious God of today. The testimony chronicled on David's staff was as important to the victory as were the stone and the sling.

The same is true for all of us. Our victories of yesterday birth in us a hope for the struggles we face today. As God encouraged Israel not to forget the miracles He performed, we, too, must clutch our testimony, refusing to relinquish it in the face of fear. The Spirit of God is still available today and God's promises are as true as ever. God is able to "do exceeding abundantly above all that we ask or think, according to the power that worketh in us" (Ephesians 3:20).

Our Testimony Encourages Future Generations

While we may be able to see the power of our testimony in connection with our everyday lives, few of us realize the power of that testimony on future generations. Long after we have laid down our testimonial staff and gone to be with the Lord, future generations can pick up that staff and discover that He is the God of Abraham, Isaac and Jacob. By examining our life, they can prove that He is faithful to all generations, that He is the God "who is, and was, and is to come" (Revelation 1:8; paraphrased).

No place in scripture better illustrates this principle than does Hebrews 11:21: "By faith Jacob, when he was a dying, blessed both the sons of Joseph; and worshipped, leaning upon the top of his staff." An old shepherd by that time, Jacob had known a mixture of heartache and victory and his staff was full of carvings that chronicled the events of his life. Ephraim and Manasseh, the sons of Joseph, knew nothing of their grandfather's journey with God, for they had been raised in Egypt, away from extended family. Even their Egyptian names revealed that Joseph, as a captive in a foreign land, had put his former life behind him. But God had proven himself faithful to Jacob and to Joseph, and had reunited father and son. What Satan had devised for destruction, God used to sustain the nation of Israel.

Joseph had longed for a day when he would once again embrace his father. But also, deep inside Joseph was a desire for Jacob to bless his sons before the patriarch died. The link between Jacob's life and the two grandsons who had grown up separated from their grandfather was the staff in Jacob's hand. As scripture indicates, Jacob blessed the sons of Joseph, leaning on the top of his staff. As he stood feebly before them, the testimony of God's faithfulness stabilized his trembling hands. Pointing to carving after carving on his staff, Jacob shared stories of the God of Abraham, and Isaac, and the same God who had proven Himself faithful in his own life. Jacob's staff gave them a history lesson while at the same time, it birthed within them a hope that God's promises to their forefathers would come to pass in their lives. The promise that their great-great-grandfather Abraham had dreamed about would become reality in their lives.

Your testimony not only enables you to win against the giants you face today, but it also stands as a beacon of light to future generations, assuring them that God is faithful and that He can be trusted. Not only is there hope of Heaven someday, but each battle we encounter carves out our short-range hope. Step by step we walk in relationship with the Lord Jesus Christ, carrying out His plan for our life and fulfilling the ultimate purpose

> *Your testimony not only enables you to win against the giants you face today, but it also stands as a beacon of light to future generations...*

for which we were created: to bring completion to the Great Commission and in doing so, hasten His return. We continue to march under the banner of Matthew 24:14: "And this gospel of the kingdom shall be preached in all the world for a witness unto all nations; and then shall the end come."

For years, I tried in vain to understand why God allowed bad things to happen to good people. In frustration I surveyed my own life, trying to put together the pieces of a puzzle that, from my perspective, made no sense. Why had my childhood been riddled with such pain and dysfunction? After all, my parents were Christians. They loved God and had done their best to serve Him.

But my problems didn't end with childhood. When I was twenty years old, my sister Alice died in the institution where she had resided for the previous eleven years. The staff of the facility described to Mom and Dad Alice's deterioration as each epileptic seizure further scarred her brain and her body became more withered. Standing in the cemetery after Alice's funeral, words seemed hollow as I held my mother's hand and saw her tears of grief drip to the ground.

Two years later, I found myself in the same cemetery, again holding Mom's hand as we laid my Dad to rest. I had more questions but fewer answers. Dad had worked hard all his life, spending forty-six years as a coal miner. Often, to provide for our family's needs he worked two shifts, back to back. But when his time to rest finally came, he didn't get to enjoy even one complete year of retirement.

I questioned why God would allow such a thing. It seemed so unfair. My father died just three months before my first child was born, and I was in need of a father more than ever, since I was learning how to be a husband and father myself. My other brothers and sisters had been able to share their joy over the birth of their children with Dad, but I would be robbed of that pleasure. Why hadn't God allowed him to live for just a few more months until I could complete a lifetime dream of showing him my son?

My father's death was followed by something more personal and life-changing. While still in my mid-twenties, I was diagnosed with thyroid cancer. Although cancer would later be ruled out, I still had to undergo a procedure that altered my life forever. To save my life, my thyroid was killed with radioactive isotope. Without thyroid regulation, my body underwent significant changes, and my weight escalated from 230 pounds to 390 pounds before the madness was stopped.

My weight gain resulted in later diagnoses of high blood pressure, diabetes, and a host of other medical problems that would leave me feeling emotionally stripped of my manhood. Eventually I found myself reduced to only ten percent of my normal energy level. Debbie had to help me dress and undress as grueling day after day dragged on. For months I felt weak and fragile as my doctors adjusted medications, trying to bring thyroid hormones levels back to normal. It seemed as if the battle for my body would never end.

On the heels of all my physical problems, Debbie became very ill as well. At first we thought she had the flu but as it lingered, it became apparent something more was wrong. After a barrage of tests, doctors informed us that she had contracted toxic shock syndrome, a dreaded disease that had taken the lives of a number of women and left many others in permanent vegetative states. Debbie's health declined quickly and she was admitted to a hospital intensive care unit, apparently only hours away from death.

Once again I found myself wrestling and bargaining with God throughout a long tension-filled night. Finally, my prayers were answered. The doctors admitted they had done all they could and that God had been involved in Debbie's recovery. She recovered completely and so did I. Only her fragile nerves and my weight problem remained; everything else returned to normal.

After our recoveries, God called us to our learning time in Texas, followed by our year of unemployment. But all of these negative events culminated on October 8, 1994, when I received a telephone call informing me that my mother had died in her sleep. Although that was the way Mom had prayed she might die, it seemed to be the straw that broke the camel's back in my life. Though I continued my daily routine, I could feel myself slipping deeper and deeper into depression. As I surveyed my life, my staff of testimony seemed to have more struggles than victories, something I soon discovered was limited vision. From God's vantage point, it was a well thought-out plan that would lead, as Esther 4:14 outlines, to my positioning for "such a time as this."

On a typical fall day in 1996, a critical piece of the puzzle of my life was put in place, opening a new door of hope and letting the light of His revelation shine through. On that day I started a new journey that in God's master plan would draw on every experience of my life. Eventually I would come to realize that the challenges of my life had not been about me after all, but rather, about His purpose and His glory.

By that time I had worked for Christian Fellowship Church over four years. A large portion of my responsibilities revolved around producing programs for our radio ministry. Secluded in a sound room, I usually worked several hours without a break. As I finished taping another broadcast, I decided to get a diet Coke from a vending machine some distance away. As I walked past an outside door, with perfect timing, the door swung open and Pastor David Parish and another man stepped inside. Senior pastor at Christian Fellowship Church for just one year, David Parish had taken over the position held by his father, J. T. Parish. Pastor David motioned for me to stop a moment and said, "Brother Rick, let me introduce you to a missionary from Kenya."

I extended my hand, prepared for a normal greeting. "Hello! Welcome to America," I said, but the missionary's response was anything but normal.

"When are you coming to Kenya?" he asked. Completely caught off guard, I found myself speechless, and just stood there, shocked. I had never entertained thoughts of traveling or of ministry outside America. Both men smiled, opened the door to Pastor's office and left me standing in the hallway baffled by the missionary's haunting question.

After a moment, I regained my composure and continued on my quest for a diet Coke. A little embarrassed by the whole encounter, I dredged my brain for reasons why I had no business in Kenya, finally settling on the excuse I would use should I face the man again. I would tell him, I decided, that I was not a missionary, nor an evangelist, but rather a teacher, and that my primary focus was training leaders. Surely that well-crafted statement would get me off the hook.

As I walked out of the room, with precise accuracy, Pastor David's office door swung open and I found myself once again face to face with the missionary. I swallowed hard but before I could offer my excuse, he spoke again, "I want you to come to Kenya and train my leaders."

For the second time, his words stripped me of a response. The two smiled again, and made their way toward an outside door, but the missionary was not quite finished with his challenge. Turning, he looked directly in my eyes, and fired a parting shot. "You will come." He stepped through the door, leaving his strange, almost prophetic, declaration still echoing in the hallway.

By that time, I felt like a boxer against the ropes, barely standing after receiving a one-two punch. I turned toward the sound room, thinking I could start again where I had left off, but that was not to be. All I heard over and over were those three words, "You will come!"

After several frustrating attempts to focus on my job in the sound room, I finally decided it was time to pray about the matter. For the next two hours, while Pastor and the missionary enjoyed their lunch, I was in the church sanctuary, wrestling with God. I could not escape the conclusion that God had been the one issuing me a challenge through the missionary, and I tried to change His mind. Questions hung over me. Would I be willing to lay aside the comforts to which I had grown accustomed? Would I be willing to leave predictable routine for an unpredictable future? I finally conceded to His will with just three words of my own, "I will go!"

Wrestling match over, I returned to my post in the sound room. God was now in control and I would leave it in His hands. He knew I was willing, but I would not be the one to push the issue. If this was His will, He was more than able to make a way. A few minutes later there was a knock at the door, and Pastor David stepped inside, alone this time. He told me of his plans to go to Kenya, and then asked the question I knew was coming, "Do you want to go with me?"

"Yes," I said as tears filled my eyes. The plan was in motion but I was scared and could hear my own heartbeat thumping in my ears. I knew absolutely nothing about the world, or Africa, or any place really. All I knew was that it was a new day, that God had intercepted my life, and that I wanted to do His will. Soon I would discover that day was just one more step in my journey of hope.

The day finally arrived when we boarded a plane for a destination halfway around the world. After an exhausting trip, I found myself in a humble village in northern Kenya. For the next three weeks, we lived in a small hut. Witnessing the lives of those precious people first hand, I looked into the faces of little children who knew only poverty, saw their mothers and fathers who wondered how they could feed and care for their children's most basic needs, saw the sick, the grieved, and the troubled. Night after night I lay awake in that hut and counted my blessings.

Finally I knew that God had allowed me to experience so much difficulty in my own life because, as I reached out to pray for the sick, I could identify with what they were feeling. Putting my arm around those grieving, I could sense their pain. And in remembering what it was like to be raised in a humble home in the mountains of Eastern Kentucky, in the ravaged-by-poverty faces of every boy and girl who passed, I saw my own face. God had allowed me to go through everything I had gone through and I was thankful, for in the difficult moments of my life compassion was birthed in me, enabling me to move from sympathy to empathy. No longer did I just feel sorry for others in their plight but I also was able to identify with them in their pain. There was, however, one major distinction between those native Kenyans and me. While I had always known of Jesus and the hope that He could bring, now God was allowing me to bring that message of hope into their hopeless situation.

I spent my forty-second birthday there in that little village, surrounded by tribal families. As I sat with them day in and day out, the words of Paul rang out in my spirit: "If in this life only we have hope, we are of all men most miserable" (I Corinthians 15:19). I saw the misery in their faces and sensed their feelings of hopelessness. In that village I determined in my heart and mind to spend the rest of my life being a carrier of this message of hope, for I realized that their greatest need was not the lack of basic provisions, but rather a Provider. They needed Jesus Christ— only He could continue to bless them long after I was gone.

As I pen these words, ten years have passed. I've been privileged to share the message of God's hope in over thirty nations, with countless thousands of people coming to Him, finding Him to be faithful in their lives as well. I have learned the value of being transparent before others, sharing with them, both privately and publicly, the struggles as well as the victories in my life. And even though countries and cultures may vary, everyone's needs are basically the same, and the message of hope in Jesus Christ remains their answer.

Two thousand years ago hope was born one day in the hearts of a handful of Jesus' disciples on the Mount of Olives. That same hope remains the focus of every believer as we become faithful disciples of Jesus. Through the mountains and valleys of our lives, we face difficulties, but each difficulty is a new opportunity for God to prove Himself faithful and true. From that proof, hope arises. We must keep our eyes fixed on Jesus and our hand firmly to the plow as we carry out the Great Commission, opening the door of hope for the hopeless, and allowing Him to build in us a short-range hope that will enable us to climb the mountain before us and all the mountains to come.

CHAPTER 9 | MY PRESENT MOUNTAIN

Jesus replied, "What does the law of Moses say? How do you read it?" The man answered, "You must love the Lord your God with all your heart, all your soul, all your strength, and all your mind." And, "Love your neighbor as yourself." "Right!" Jesus told him. "Do this and you shall live!" (Luke 10:26–28; NLT)

Although actually responding to a skeptic's trick question, the answer Jesus gave is a recipe for an abundant and eternal life. For me, this passage has also taken on new meaning as I recover from dysfunction. I've been a Christian more than thirty years, but until recently had obeyed only one-fourth of Jesus' instruction in this scripture. Although I loved God with all my heart, I unintentionally ignored Him with my soul (emotions), my strength (physical body), and my mind (intellect). Even though He had my heart, I remained an emotional disaster and a physical wreck, living with the mental anguish of knowing what I should be doing while continuing in self-destructive patterns that were sure to bring me to an early grave.

In this chapter and the next, we are going to shift direction slightly to deal with issues of recovery and wholeness in our lives. Everyone, it seems, has been scarred by pain and injustice received at the hands of others, especially during childhood by family members and authority figures. These scars caused by dysfunctional relationships can prevent us from moving forward into the best God has for our lives and our ministry for Him.

The greatest struggles an individual faces in overcoming

dysfunction revolve around their own beliefs, how they see themselves—their "self-portrait" if you will. How we see ourselves determines how we respond in various situations. Sad to say, our history becomes the obstacle to our destiny, and we feel helpless to rise above our self-portrait.

But the Word of God is the key, opening the door to a new destiny. God, and God alone, is able to paint a new picture of us, and as we believe in the new portrait that His view of us establishes, the limits are removed from our lives. We must take the brush out of the hands of people and place it in the hands of God, for in Him we become new creatures. When we do this, the past is put behind us, and the future becomes new before us. Our hope of a new beginning can only be found in the One who is able to erase the past.

> *How WE SEE OURSELVES DETERMINES HOW WE RESPOND IN VARIOUS SITUATIONS.*

A dysfunctional environment hampers individuals in so many ways. Without realizing it, those raised in dysfunction usually respond in one of three ways as adults: 1) they find someone to treat them as they have always been treated; 2) they treat others as they were treated; or 3) they treat themselves as they have always been treated. Let's look at each of these in turn.

They find someone to treat them as they have always been treated.

This explains why abused children grow up to marry abusers. For them, abuse is normal, and the low self-image resulting from that abuse sabotages any hope of change or future happiness. As people evaluate their lives, they come to the conclusion that the abuse they receive is their fault, and that they must deserve it. This self-perception becomes truth to such people, causing them to be drawn to whatever their particular dysfunction might be, going from one abusive relationship to another, for example, or from one alcoholic to another. Like a robot, their minds have been programmed and their actions carry out that programming. They are in the clutches of a mental stronghold.

The word "stronghold" can be defined as "a house constructed of thoughts that hold us captive." Imprisoned by an improper mindset, it is impossible for people to change their actions unless they are first willing or able to change their mind. An elephant chained to a stake when very young learns that pulling against the chain is fruitless. Years later, although that small chain is no longer a match for the adult elephant's strength, it still binds him. In reality, although the chain is not strong enough to hold the giant animal, he is now imprisoned by his thoughts concerning the chain. The animal becomes convinced that nothing will ever change.

They treat others as they were treated.

Another manner in which those raised in the trauma of dysfunction operate later is to treat others as they themselves have been treated. They become perpetual victims, allowing pent up anger and pain to become weapons that inflict pain on those around them, even on those sincerely trying to reach out in love to help. Refusing to deal with their pain, they keep rehearsing it, building a stronger and stronger case against the world. Like a seriously injured dog, they snap at everyone. Their negative actions cause others to fear and reject them, a complicating situation that exacerbates the problem. Each rejection brings more pain and more anger, and on and on the vicious cycle continues until the individual is completely out of control. If they do not allow some type of intervention, they will eventually snap and hurt people who were completely uninvolved in their pain.

All of us have heard and seen extreme forms of this behavior on news programs. Some poor soul, emotionally scarred by a life of dysfunction, is laid off from his job along with a number of other employees. Yet to him, the layoff is a personal attack. He reacts by going home, loading a gun, and returning to the work site where he fires indiscriminately on his fellow employees, wounding and killing innocent people. The truth is that the crisis event was only one situation in a lifetime of emotional battering, but it was enough to push the individual over an edge.

As news reporters interview witnesses and those close to the tragedy, people who knew the assailant always seem to have the same response: "He seemed like a nice guy, just a normal fellow." That's exactly right! This was normal for him. Accustomed to being on the receiving end of violent behavior, he followed a pattern of coping by venting his personal pain through acts of violent behavior. Rather than properly dealing with his pain, he found it easier to blame others and lash out in revenge. Such a person always sees himself as a victim; the world is against him and everyone is out to destroy him.

People like this have been programmed by the pain of childhood or some particular event in their life when someone used them or hurt them and destroyed the positive image they had of themselves. While their pain and feelings of injustice were valid at that time, even though those days are gone, the memory of the pain remains. Now that they are adults, because the pain is still real, they cannot stop reacting to it. In order for those people to change their future, they must take responsibility, and act instead of reacting. We cannot live our lives successfully in defensive mode; we must go on the offense if we expect to have a productive future.

They treat themselves as they have always been treated.

This method of operation describes my response to dysfunction. I became self-destructive. Others perceived me as a great guy, full of compassion and love. I had an ideal mate to enjoy life with, my children were wonderful, and I was the envy of all. My friends were loyal and committed because I treated them with loyalty and respect. Yet, I still had one enemy and that enemy was me! The self-portrait I carried was one of low self-image and unworthiness. I hated myself; therefore, I couldn't properly receive love from God, from my companion, my family, or my friends.

When I considered my childhood, laced as it was with dysfunction and favoritism, I came to the conclusion that my dad was right in not having anything to do with me and that I didn't deserve his time or attention. After all, I had taken the blame for things in my family that I had nothing to do with. I could not prevent all that had happened to them, for most of their pain occurred even before I was born. But no matter how hard I tried to impress or please my dad, my efforts seemed to go wrong. While trying to hoe the weeds, I cut down the corn. While trying to trim the hedges, I cut the electrical cord in two. If I hit a rock while mowing, it crashed through a window. It seemed that whenever I tried, I failed, and my father's reaction was always the same—anger. He usually slapped my face or sent me to my room, actions that reinforced my feelings of rejection. So, in my mind I came to believe that I deserved to be labeled a failure. There was plenty of evidence to back up that label. I was a klutz who took clumsiness to a new level.

After trying to gain my dad's acceptance and failing over and over again, I became disillusioned with the whole process. My feelings of rejection became the seeds for a harvest of destruction. I found myself driven to candy, which offered a few moments of sweet relief. No matter how bad I felt inside, it seemed that a candy bar or two soothed my emotions and gave me the courage to try again.

Of course, my secret candy indulgence could not stay hidden for long as I began putting on weight. Throughout grade school, I was the chubbiest kid in class and by the time I reached junior high school, I had topped 200 pounds. More disgusted with myself than ever, I soothed my emotions with more candy, the only way I knew to respond. By the beginning of my junior year in high school my weight had climbed to 297 pounds with no end in sight. I was miserable and firmly stuck in a destructive pattern.

But as my junior year of high school began, I met a teacher who gave me reprieve from a lifetime of pain and whose influence would change my life forever. Her name was Mattie Knight and she taught speech and drama at our school. How ironic that God would use a teacher to start a process of restoration within me. Ever since eighth grade when a teacher physically abused me, I had been turned off to the entire educational system. But Mrs. Knight gave me hope for a better tomorrow. Although one teacher had brought me pain, this one would bring gain.

Since I hated school and sought the easiest way through,

I signed up to take her class because I had been told it was easy. When I entered Mrs. Knight's classroom, I expected to be greeted with what I called a teacher's New Year Speech. It would go something like this: "I know who you are, and I've heard of all the trouble that you have caused in other classes. I want you to know that I'm in charge of this class, and I will not tolerate you bringing chaos to my classroom. Do you understand me?" I would always look at the teacher with a smirk on my face, thinking to myself, "We'll see how long this lasts, sister. You haven't seen the trouble I can cause you."

But, as I strolled into Mrs. Knight's classroom, she looked up from her desk, a smile gracing her face, and in a chipper voice, she said, "Well, hello there young man." I smiled back, thinking that she must not have recognized me.

"Do you know how special you are?" I shrugged my shoulders, totally astonished at her question and muttered, "No."

"Well, you are anyway, whether you know it or not," she stated. "God has a very special place for you in life and I'm going to see that you get there." I didn't know what to say and just stood there. No doubt, she could see the shock on my face. "From now on," she continued, "I'm going to call you Baby. That's your new nickname. You're my Baby." Mrs. Knight had only one child, ironically named Babydoll; now I, apparently, was being adopted as 'Baby.'

"Is that okay with you?" she asked and I said, "Sure."

"You're going to be the white sheep in my family," she laughed and I laughed, too, sharing the joke with her since Mrs. Knight was black. Never before had I felt such acceptance and love. Although I didn't know how long it would last, man it felt wonderful having someone think I was special and that

I had a place where I could fit in. I knew that she genuinely believed in me.

Mrs. Knight's investment in my life over the next two years prepared me for a lifetime of public speaking. It also resulted in my winning various awards in state competitions. Although being constantly on stage forced me to confront my physical appearance, Mrs. Knight never once referred to my size. I just wanted to be my best so she would be proud of me.

By the time I graduated high school, my accomplishments in speech and drama had earned me popularity. I had also lost seventy-two pounds, was physically fit, and excited about living. But even though things had changed outwardly, I was unaware of the emotional pain still residing in the recesses of my mind. But one thing was certain—through speech and drama I learned how to mask my pain and to act as if everything was wonderful. That act would continue as part of my life's drama for the next thirty years.

When I became a Christian shortly after getting out of high school, I called Mrs. Knight to inform her of the news. She was overjoyed! She congratulated me and I could hear her voice breaking over the phone as she told me how she had been praying for me, and she knew that God's plan was being set in motion for my life.

But even so I struggled to relate to God properly. After all, I had never been successful in pleasing my earthly father, and I wasn't certain I could please my Heavenly Father either. Even though I did all the things that proper Christians do, feelings of acceptance eluded me, leaving me empty inside, causing me to return to the candy for soothing.

I was active in sports at that time so I was able to keep

my weight maintained and cover my addiction to sweets, but I still didn't know how to fill the emotional void and receive the healing I needed. Like a carrot dangled before a donkey in order to keep it moving forward, the prize of wholeness seemed beyond my reach. My life was almost normal, but not quite.

Dad and I both learned lessons from our lives, and before his death established a better relationship, but I still didn't feel that he was pleased with me. I lacked the affirmation necessary to deal with my pain.

After my dad's death I faced the thyroid condition I mentioned earlier. The treatment for that condition devastated me emotionally and changed my physical appearance as well. Hit in my two weakest areas—emotional and physical—the crisis triggered an increased desire for the comforts of candy and sweets; they became the crutch I leaned on during those times of instability. With my mind and physical body completely out of whack, my addiction to sweets was the only thing that seemed normal.

Once again, my weight began to reveal my secret. Climbing steadily, it finally reached a new level that I had never before known—390 pounds! But I felt I had a legitimate excuse in that I had lost my thyroid and the weight gain was not my fault. Every time I felt the sting of rejection, I retreated to more and more candy to soothe my emotional pain. Candy, though, only made my problems worse because by that time, I had also developed diabetes and was taking insulin to stabilize my blood sugar levels. Although I had to have it to ease my emotional pain, the sugar in candy required more and more insulin in order to avoid the life-threatening effects of unstable blood sugar levels. I know my behavior may seem bizarre to you, but having practiced that pattern of behavior since age five, it was life as normal for me.

Ministry only added to the stress of my physical problems. Pulled by a busy schedule and the demands of people, I learned to live on junk food, grabbing a doughnut here and a candy bar there as I ran from one person in need to another, trying to be super pastor. It seemed I had an answer to everyone's need but my own. In guilt I thought of myself as a hypocrite because I knew that regardless of my thyroid excuse, people knew that I had problems I was unwilling to face. But, because of my love and compassion for people, others chose to look past my problem as I slowly committed suicide with food. In a life that was truly spiraling out of control, I soothed my guilty emotions with even more candy.

As I traveled, preached and prayed for people, I told them that Jesus had the answer for every problem they faced. Then after others were encouraged and lifted up, I returned to an empty motel room, physically exhausted and emotionally spent. There I would lie on the bed with a bag of candy in one hand and a book in the other, getting my fix.

I recall one night when I was alone in a motel room, reading a book about the fall of a great evangelist. Like me, he also had been raised in dysfunction and his crutch had become whiskey. He preached meeting after meeting, each time returning to his motel room where he drank whiskey until he passed out. He actually died drunk, in a motel room, after preaching a message of hope to thousands of people. I shook my head in amazement, took another bite of candy, and flipped the page, refusing to admit that I was just like that man. The only difference was that my addiction was acceptable in the religious world and his was not. But like him, I was also on a crash course toward death.

My ridiculous behavior continued week after week, month after month, year after year. Well skilled in laughing off the seriousness of the situation, I offered one funny quip or another to anyone who mentioned my weight problem. As for me, I wouldn't allow myself to think about it. My focus remained on getting others well and in doing all I could to get them to love me. Somehow I justified my indulgence of the flesh. After all, didn't I deserve this one thing since I was giving everything else to God and others? All I had left was eating, I reasoned; surely, God would understand.

Just like the evangelist in the book I read, I had experienced several close calls. On more than one occasion I recall waking up drenched in sweat and in insulin shock. Having eaten all the candy I could hold, I would then try to estimate how much insulin it would take to balance out the ride. Apparently, several times I overestimated and took too much insulin, which caused my sugar levels to plummet too low. I was playing medical Russian roulette, hoping that it wouldn't kill me.

One night, feeling unusually lonely and depressed after preaching a meeting in Corbin, Kentucky, I purchased a couple bags of candy at a nearby convenience store and polished them off while watching television alone in my motel room. All that sugar caused me to become sleepy and lethargic, so I decided to go to bed. But first I did my insulin thing. Apparently, I wasn't thinking clearly and I took far too much insulin.

I awoke in the middle of the night in serious trouble. My vision was a blur and I could barely walk. Knowing that I needed more sugar to get my insulin levels up, I threw on pants and a shirt and staggered into the hallway, trying to make it to a vending machine. Even though I thought I was walking normally, I felt my head hit first one side of the hallway and then the other. Finally reaching the vending machines at the end of the hallway, I struggled desperately to get the money into the slot. Thank God, there were coins in my pocket; without them my life might have ended that night in that hallway.

Leaning against the wall, I ate the candy necessary to balance my blood sugar levels. Gradually my vision returned, and as my sugar levels rose, I felt my body readjusting. When I made my way back to my room and looked at the bed, where I had lain was an outline of my body in sweat. I thought of the chalk outlines police use to identify the place where dead bodies were found. With a knot in the pit of my stomach, I realized I had almost killed myself. Tears dripped from my cheeks as I sat on the side of the bed. Although it was only 3 a.m., I sat there the rest of the night, unable to go back to sleep, unnerved by what had occurred.

That event served as one of the turning points God used to bring me toward recovery. I wish I could tell you that I immediately changed my behavior and that my foolishness never happened again, but that was not the case. What I can tell you is that, from that point on, I knew for certain that I had a serious problem and that unless I changed, someday it would result in my death.

That incident was the first of three events that would bring me to a point of dealing with my problem. In a baseball analogy, it was Strike One. Strike Two occurred on August 19, 2004, with the birth of our first grandchild. Strike Three was less than two months away. It occurred on October 3, 2004, and I'll tell you about that experience in detail in the next chapter.

The birth of Richard Dale Clendenen III, whom we call "Trey," was my second wake-up call. One of the most precious moments of my life was when I stood in the hospital hallway next to my son who beamed with pride as he held his son in his arms. Then suddenly a sobering thought struck my mind, "I'm not going to live to see this child grow up unless I deal with this problem." The thought of such a thing cut deep like a knife. I recalled the absence of my father at Richie's birth. Was I going to allow Trey to grow up only knowing me through the stories of others?

God was doing everything He could to get my attention and He finally did through the words of my son. Having the same feelings I had felt as a young father, Richie said, "Dad, it's time to make a change. I don't want you to die. I want you around to put your fingerprints on this little boy." I realized that Richie had also missed knowing my Dad, and I couldn't allow history to repeat itself with my grandson.

At that moment I realized there was a lot at stake, but as crazy as it sounds, I still didn't know where to begin. I had been on every kind of diet imaginable and had even invented some of my own. But they never worked over the long haul. It was then that I began to consider having gastric bypass surgery, thinking perhaps it could be my answer.

Three things made gastric bypass surgery an appealing option. First, I was told that after surgery it was impossible to overeat, even if one wanted to. I was also told that eating anything with sugar, if it didn't kill you, would make you wish you were dead because it would make you so sick. I even talked to several "sugaraholics" for whom bypass surgery helped them break the habit. Finally, I hoped that surgery would provide a legitimate excuse for me to give to my family and friends. Enablers to my eating addiction, they offered me cakes and candy to demonstrate their love. Most of my life had been lived out in social gatherings, family get-togethers, and church suppers where, under the label of fellowship, we gorged ourselves in unhealthy eating. On one hand, people were concerned about my health and afraid that I might die. On the other hand, they pressed another slice of chocolate cake on me and would not take no for an answer.

My search for a solution finally led me to my family doctor and friend of over twenty years who also suffered with a weight problem. He told me he was having gastric bypass and went on to say that he would blaze a trail for me to follow. Since I was more than 100 pounds overweight and had been diagnosed with all four diseases that justified gastric bypass, he was willing to recommend me for surgery. I breathed a sigh of relief thinking that soon my ordeal would be over. Just a few stitches and a lifetime of pain would melt away.

But my insurance company refused to approve me for gastric bypass surgery unless I was first willing to undergo a twelve-week supervised weight loss program that included diet and exercise, plus a psychological evaluation and group therapy. Devastated when I received their letter of rejection, I felt hopeless. Even though I was certain I would fail at some point in the twelve weeks and sabotage the process, I had no other choice. I was convinced that I could not lose weight alone.

When I arrived at the Centennial Obesity Clinic to begin

the process, I admit that I felt ashamed that as a preacher my life choices had brought me to that point. My first appointment was with a dietician, Jill, who was very kind and considerate of my feelings. She talked to me about eating to live instead of living to eat.

From Jill's office, Debbie and I made our way down a hall to talk with Brian, a physiologist. He talked to me about exercise and explained that our bodies were designed for activity and that, in my line of work, I was not getting nearly enough. We came to an agreement of what would be expected of me over the next few weeks. Truthfully, my experience at the clinic to that point was the easy part—the difficult part was at our next appointment.

With Debbie by my side, we entered the room where group therapy took place. Psychologist Dr. Evelyn Frye conducted the group therapy sessions that, I had already decided, would be a complete waste of my time. After all, I thought that my problem was my weight, not my mind. But because group therapy was required, I reluctantly took a seat among the ten others gathered there. Dr. Frye entered the room and greeted us with a smile and a cheerful hello. Then she explained the rules that would govern our therapy sessions. I listened intently but had already made up my mind not to speak unless spoken to.

For the next hour, I sat there, hiding my feelings and listening as one after another of those in attendance described struggles like those I had battled my entire life. It seemed that everything they said applied to my life in one area or another and I was amazed.

Suddenly Dr. Frye looked at my name tag, focused her

attention on me, and asked, "Rick, why are you here?" I responded by telling her about my insurance problem and that I had been forced into this twelve week program.

She wasted no time confronting me with a second question, "Do you know what your problem is?" When I politely responded, "No, ma'am" she said, "Well, I do. You are full of anger." I could feel my face flush with anger and I forced a smile to cover my true feelings. But she had touched a nerve and I knew it.

She went on to explain that trauma causes pain and the emotional response to pain is anger. She said that obesity comes later as we try to cover that anger with enough fat to keep it hidden. But, she assured me, as my weight began to melt away the anger would surface and I would be forced to deal with issues that had caused the problem.

I was offended at her audacity in telling me—a well-respected preacher of the Gospel—that I had an anger problem. But then, of course, she didn't know I was a preacher and I'm not sure it would have made a difference anyway. All she knew was that my name was Rick and that since I was in the group, apparently I had a problem.

I fumed all the way home from Nashville, Tennessee, trying to forget that statement. Surely, she was wrong. I wasn't full of anger. Yes, I was willing to admit that I had a problem, but my problem was with weight, not anger.

Just a week later, I found myself back in Nashville. This time, I was gathered with my brothers and sisters at the hospital bedside of my brother, Tom, who was having problems with his heart. We were there to support him. As Tom was rolled away to an operating room, someone suggested eating breakfast since all of us had left our homes early and the time was approaching 10 a.m. Now on a dietary schedule, I had already eaten breakfast, and it was too early for lunch. But I agreed to go with them and have a cup a coffee as they ate.

The blessing over the food ended with a unified 'Amen' and everyone began eating, except me. Suddenly I felt myself becoming tense and very nervous. The longer I sat there, the worse I felt, and my nervousness turned to anger. Why? Nothing had been said to provoke me. The conversation around the table was pleasant and light as we reminisced about old times. My anger finally escalated to the point where I could no longer remain in my chair and I excused myself from the table. While others thought I was going to the restroom, the truth was I just needed to be alone.

I walked up and down the hospital hallway, trying to figure out why I was angry. I even stepped outside for fresh air, thinking that perhaps I was just feeling the tension of the moment. Then like a bolt of lightning, I had a flashback. I saw myself at five years old, sitting with my family around the table. My place was just to the left of Dad, directly across the table from Mom. My brothers Tom and Butch were across the table on Mom's side a bit to my left.

The family table is intended to be a peaceful place of fellowship, but ours was anything but peaceful. Like a movie playing in my mind, I recalled a scene that occurred three or four nights each week. Dad was a very serious man, and he allowed no nonsense at the table. We were expected to march in like little soldiers and sit quietly while eating. But, prompted by jealously stemming from my favored relationship with Mom, my brothers Tom and Butch did everything they could to make me laugh. Eventually they succeeded and I laughed out loud. When I did, Dad exploded in anger, slapped me across the face, and sent me with plate in hand to the living room. There I joined Alice on the stairs to the second story of our house, eating my supper and crying while Butch and Tom smirked. That scene was repeated over and over throughout my childhood.

Forty-five years later, again gathered with my family around a table, the anger I had suppressed in childhood surfaced. While I thought I was losing my mind, in fact I was actually taking my first step on a long journey to recovery. For years, I fed my buried feelings candy to keep them dormant, never allowing myself to really examine my feelings or process the pain that lay beneath them. But in the computer of my mind, the information had been filed away; that day's events hit a button that flashed them to the screen.

Suddenly I realized that for forty-five years, on every occasion when I gathered with my brothers and sisters, I fed my emotions by stuffing them into silence with candy. But this time, I had no candy to offer, and my emotions roared in protest. After a few minutes of prayer and processing, I returned to the table. No one there knew what had taken place within me, but I was now fully aware that there was a lot more I needed to deal with.

Everything went well with Tom after his surgery, and the Clendenen brothers and sisters returned to our homes and regular routines. But I couldn't get the therapy group out of my mind. Although my scheduled return to the group was two weeks away, I made plans to attend early, not because of some outward requirement forced on me, but because of an inward need driving me to understand myself more and to learn how to get over the feelings I was carrying. Two weeks was too long to keep the secrets inside. Since Dr. Frye had already predicted that my anger would surface, and it had happened as she had said it would, I knew she could help. She was obviously a lot smarter than I had given her credit for being. Something inside me was screaming to get out and I decided that, regardless of whether or not the bypass surgery ever took place, I would not give up until every shelf in my mind was clean and I was whole.

As Dr. Frye began the group therapy session, she seemed a little shocked that I was present ahead of my required attendance. But she welcomed me, and said it was good to see me. I confessed how angry I had been after the first group therapy session then went on to say that everything she had said would happen, had happened. She smiled and asked the same question she had asked two weeks before, "Why are you here today?" My response this time was completely different and I replied, "Because I know that only the truth will set me free and I am willing to face the truth now regardless of how ugly it seems."

Immediately she responded to that statement with another challenge: "Then we are going to have to deal with your unforgiveness, your desire to control everyone, and your judgmentalism."

"Give me a break, lady!" I thought. "Can't we at least take a day or two to rest?" But I held my peace and for the next two hours, I listened and learned what was ahead of me on my journey to wholeness.

My journey to wholeness has required me to examine the health of all my relationships. Some relationships have required new boundaries. For

> *MY JOURNEY TO WHOLENESS HAS REQUIRED ME TO EXAMINE THE HEALTH OF ALL MY RELATIONSHIPS.*

example, I felt it necessary to meet with Tom and Butch to discuss the conduct that had caused me continual pain since childhood. I admitted my anger; they admitted their jealousy. Together we have forged a new relationship that is stronger than ever.

Step by step, in meeting after meeting, I have learned who and how to forgive. I've stopped blaming other people, taking personal responsibility for my own future. I've learned how to show mercy, even to those who hurt me out of their own pain. In my efforts to leave no stone unturned, I have made many new and painful discoveries. But through it all, I have also felt God supplying the grace necessary to resolve the issues that had me bound. I am becoming more and more whole, and increasingly under His lordship and His leadership.

Finally, I am learning to love Him with all my heart, soul, mind, and strength. His grace is painting a new portrait of me inside my mind, and I am learning to love myself. As a result, I am witnessing my love for others grow stronger and stronger. Now I realize why I had struggled to love my neighbor—it was because I didn't love myself.

Just as God calls all of us to our next mountaintop of victory, I have learned to lift my hands in humble surrender to His perfect will for my life. My prayer has become, "Lord, please make me whole in spirit, soul and body. In turn, I will be able to love my neighbor as myself and extend my hand to aid them in climbing the mountains they face in their own journey. Amen"

CHAPTER 10 | MOUNTAIN LIVING

SO THERE IS A FULL COMPLETE REST STILL WAITING FOR THE PEOPLE OF GOD. CHRIST HAS ALREADY ENTERED THERE. HE IS RESTING FROM HIS WORK, JUST AS GOD DID AFTER THE CREATION. (HEBREWS 4:9–10; NIV)

"A full complete rest still waiting..."—how inviting those words sound in a world of constant hustle and bustle. Aside from the outward pressures of everyday life, we also wrestle inwardly, trying to piece together the puzzles of our individual lives. Shaped by our environment, experiences, and educational backgrounds, it seems we spend the rest of our lives comparing ourselves against everyone around us in search of that elusive thing called normal. We lose sight of God's goal of excellence for our lives and settle for just blending in. If we can reach a point where others do not consider us weird or strange, that, in itself, seems to offer a comfortable substitute for wholeness. But God has created us for more.

God calls us to live on a higher plane and prepares us for mountain living. He purchased, with His own Son, all that we would ever need to enter into the rest He has in mind. He also surrounds us with the people we will need to support us on the journey. But there is a price to be paid to enter the rest of God and it requires ceasing from our own labor. It is difficult for us to learn to trust Him fully. Instead,

> GOD CALLS US TO LIVE ON A HIGHER PLANE AND PREPARES US FOR MOUNTAIN LIVING.

we daily demonstrate our unbelief by continuing our feeble efforts to attain what, by His grace, He has already given us. We must learn to fall into His arms of love and rest.

We are often like a drowning man who flails and splashes in a panicked attempt to save himself. Even though rescuers are nearby, they cannot safely approach without risking harm to themselves, so the panicked person actually prevents himself from being rescued. We just can't bring ourselves to a place of trust and instead, with all that is within us, try to save ourselves. The truth of the matter is, like a flailing drowning person, we don't need to be saved from the water, but instead need to be saved from ourselves and from foolish behavior that will end in death.

Throughout this book I have endeavored to be brutally honest with you concerning my life. I have shared mountaintop experiences, as well as many of the valleys. I have openly shared my dysfunctional upbringing, as well as my attempt to cope with those dysfunctions by turning to food rather than to God. I have written without a fig leaf, so to speak, in hopes that my story would not have to be repeated in your life through destructive behavior.

What I am about to share with you now is in some ways, the most difficult story of all. It occurred on October 3, 2004, and is the pivotal moment of my life. It is the Strike Three I mentioned in the previous chapter. On one hand what I experienced that night was sobering in that I saw the final results of a lifetime of destructive behavior. On the other hand, it birthed a hope for change that time has not diminished. I suppose my greatest fear in sharing this experience with you is the possibility of judgment that may follow. As human beings, our natural tendency is to evaluate others and judge their credibility based on their worst, or occasionally their best, moment while ignoring the events of their lives that brought them to that point. I'm sure the same will be true for me as I share this particular event with you.

Though I have faithfully served the Lord for over thirty years, preaching the Gospel in some thirty-four nations of the world, most of those who know me best would characterize my life and ministry with one word—balance. I'm a middle of the road kind of guy with a middle of the road kind of ministry. Throughout my life I have tried diligently not to be viewed as a flake. Yet what I am about to share with you may seem far-fetched. But I can assure you that it happened exactly as I write it today and I trust the Holy Spirit to affirm its validity to your heart.

As a traveling minister I relied on sweets to sustain me emotionally while I maintained a daily schedule that most people would deem insane. Already exhausted from a year of speaking engagements, I found myself scheduled to visit South Africa in September of 2004. My itinerary called for me to preach twenty-one times in an eighteen-day period, while traveling by car across the nation. At that time in my life I was unaccustomed to considering the physical strain such a plan would pose for me. I was in complete denial concerning my physical needs. I was on a quest to prove my value through productivity.

While preparing for the South Africa trip, I received a phone call from a precious friend who asked if I could preach in his place one Sunday. As I looked through my calendar, I realized that the Sunday he was requesting was the weekend I would be returning from South Africa. As the only time available between my South Africa trip and my U.S. traveling schedule, I had set aside that weekend for some rest because I knew I would be exhausted after the trip.

As I waited for a pause in the conversation so I could graciously decline his invitation, he told me the reason he wanted me to preach for him. That particular Sunday, he said, would be the first anniversary of the death of his twelve-year old grandson who had been killed in a tragic car accident. His voice broke as he explained that he felt my visit would not only help the church cope with the loss, but would also strengthen his own family through a difficult time. By that time we were both crying, and with compassion winning over wisdom, I told him he could count on me to be there. As I hung up the phone, though, I felt a knot in the pit of my stomach and knew that I was overextending myself. But how could I say no? After all, what are friends for?

The trip to South Africa was stressful enough in itself with long flights and layovers. Then the schedule that awaited me once I arrived was more than enough to kill a healthy man, and I was anything but healthy. Although my time in South Africa was productive, I was completely exhausted when Debbie met me at the airport in Nashville, Tennessee. Looking at my watch, I counted the hours until I needed to be back on the road again. Then I reminded Debbie that we needed to leave early the next morning for my friend's church in St. Louis, Missouri.

Debbie's response was to tell me I was crazy and that God wanted me to live for Him instead of killing myself for Him. I smiled and assured her that I would be fine.

We made it through that challenging weekend but it left me not only physically wasted, but emotionally spent as well. I found myself once again with my scheduling calendar in hand, trying to find time for rest, but nothing was available. Helping my friend in need had used up the only rest slot available. In the week that lay before me, two trips were planned, and the following weekend I was to be the guest speaker at a church in Cape Girardeau, Missouri. As Debbie glanced at my calendar, she asked, "When are you going to get some rest?" I tried to laugh it off and replied, "Aw, I can rest when I get to Heaven."

After a busy week of running, on Saturday, October 2, 2004, we drove to Cape Girardeau, arriving late in the evening. After grabbing a quick bite to eat, we headed to our motel room for a night of rest before my next preaching engagement. Suddenly I began shaking inside, a sensation that made me feel as if my insides were coming to the outside. When I held out my hands, they were steady, but I was helpless to stop the jerking within, and thought perhaps I was experiencing some kind of panic attack. After all, I hadn't exactly been taking care of myself. I took a few deep breaths, trying to bring calm.

Finally, not able to keep my distress hidden, I told Debbie, "Something is wrong with me." She reached into our luggage for the medical bag that made us look like doctors instead of preachers, and began checking my blood sugar levels. They were normal, at least for me. My blood pressure was also fine. There was no apparent reason for what I was experiencing, but believe me, I knew something wasn't right.

I could tell the whole situation was unnerving to Debbie and she suggested, "Maybe we should go to the emergency room." But I responded, "No. We just need to go to bed. I've most likely just hit the wall. Nothing a good night's sleep won't help." So we turned out the lights. As I laid there in the dark, shaking inside, I quietly asked God to touch me as I drifted off to sleep. I never expected Him to answer my prayer quite the way He did.

I don't know how long I had been asleep when I felt myself ascending upward. It was dark just for a moment and then it turned as bright as noonday. A large mountain loomed before me, and without human effort, I began to glide up that mountain, feeling as though I were floating six to eight inches above the ground. I was not afraid at all; in fact, I was at perfect peace and fully aware of everything around me.

As I crested the mountain, I found myself standing in a hallway outside a courtroom, not sure of how I had arrived there. "What is this? Where am I?" I asked myself.

Looking around, I noticed that the walls were beautifully carved wood and the floors were white marble—a gorgeous sight. Suddenly from behind me, a voice announced, "The Lord Jesus is in the courtroom," and I wondered if I should go in or wait to be called in.

Like metal shavings drawn to a magnet, I felt my heart being pulled toward the courtroom and I glided to a point just inside the doorway. Looking toward the front of the room, I was surprised that the courtroom had no furnishings, only a white marble floor. Before me in the courtroom was a judge's bench like nothing I had ever seen. Standing around twelve feet high, it was beyond beautiful, but it was also empty.

But where was Jesus? Part of the room was obstructed from my view by the door, so I continued into the room moving to the far right-hand wall. Then, as I turned to face the bench, I noticed what appeared to be a judge's chambers to my right. The door to that chamber was open and Jesus sat inside at a desk, as if He were in counsel.

When I saw Him, the strangest thing occurred. The Jesus inside of me cried out to the Jesus in front of me. I could not contain His name and it erupted from my spirit like a volcano. As His name rang out, He leaped to His feet and ran toward me like a mother responding to the cry of her own baby. I made my way toward Him, and we embraced in the middle of the courtroom.

He was nothing like I imagined He would look. His shoulder length hair was curly and as black as coal. His nose was very large and pronounced, and to my surprise, He had no beard. He stood about six foot two and wore a black robe like those traditionally worn by judges. But those things were insignificant compared to being in His arms with my head resting on His right shoulder and His head on my shoulder.

Thought after thought raced through my mind. What am I supposed to say? What am I supposed to do? After all, this is God! He knows everything I've ever done, every thought I've ever had. So I started saying, "I love You, Jesus. I love You so much!" Over and over, I repeated my love for Him. In our way of judging time, I suppose a minute and a half to two minutes passed without any response from Him. One thing stood out to me during that moment and I don't know how or why I knew it—my works were being judged. I was not at all concerned about my salvation for I knew that He was living in me and for the first time in my life I understood the scripture, "Christ in you, the hope of glory" (Colossians 1:27). But somehow, as I continued to affirm my love over and over, I knew that His judgment of my works would determine my station in Heaven.

Then He moved His hands from my back to my shoulders and stepped back. Looking me straight in the face, as a father would look at his son in order to tell him something important, He said, "I believe you really do love Me." I embraced Him again, this time with my head on His left shoulder and His head on my left shoulder. "With all my heart, I love You, Lord," I responded. Over and over, I told Him how much I loved Him as another minute or two passed with us standing together.

Then I felt Him move lean back and His hair brushed against the left side of my face. I actually thought He was going to say something into my ear when He suddenly kissed me on my left cheek and said, "Then go back and do your best for Me." With that statement, He vanished from my arms.

The next thing I share with you I'm certain sounds strange, but my very next realization was that I had no arms. Although I had been embracing Jesus, and it felt like a hug, I didn't have arms. Looking down, I realized that I also didn't have a body. I couldn't fathom how that could be for I had felt His hands on my back, His hair touch my skin, and even His kiss on my cheek. Yet, amazingly, I didn't have a body!

Body or no, suddenly I felt a hand grasp my upper left arm and a tug turned me around to look into the face of an angel. His hair was dark and cut short to a face that was without facial hair. He wore a blue tunic. The angel smiled at me and without one word being spoken, I fully understood that it was time to go. He turned and started gliding down the mountain with me traveling about twelve to eighteen inches in his wake.

I strained to catch another glimpse of the angel's face because I had never seen one before, but then something else caught my attention. As we descended the mountain I saw a crowd of hundreds of people coming up the mountain toward us. Although I could see their features and even the color of their clothing, I also looked directly through them to the mountain behind. I suppose that is what I must have looked like to them as well. As we came to the crowd, the angel stretched out his hand like Moses at the Red Sea, and the crowd parted like water before us as we continued our descent.

At the bottom of the mountain was a flat grassy field. Suddenly, I saw two gates. Rounded at the top and very ugly, the gates had been white at one time, but had faded to an unappealing, dingy gray. We approached them at a speed three to four times faster than a person can run. The angel zipped through the gates and, since I knew I didn't have a body, I expected to go through them without any difficulty as well. But when I hit those gates, the abrupt impact was like running into a wall at full force. First I felt my feet, then my legs, then my torso, and finally my head. I felt my body become rigid and lift off the bed. And although it felt as though the breath had been knocked out of me, the opposite was true. With force, I exhaled a full breath of air and sat straight up in bed. I was back on the motel bed in Cape Girardeau. Strangely, at that exact moment a car alarm outside our room blared three times, then stopped. Debbie shouted in the darkness, "Rick, are you all right?"

Quickly I struggled to compose myself and muttered, "I'm fine. Go back to sleep." I knew that if I said anything to Debbie she would be asking questions the rest of the night.

Curiously, I was not one bit afraid or nervous. In fact, the shaking in my body was gone and I felt a peace like I had never felt before. I rolled over in bed and told the Lord again, silently, how much I loved Him and went to sleep, sleeping like a baby through what remained of the night.

When morning came, Debbie was full of questions and wanted to know what had happened to me during the night. As she sat on the side of the bed, I explained the whole event in detail.

As I told Debbie, I don't know if what I experienced that

night was a dream, a vision, or my own death. Deep down I believe I died that night. One thing is certain—I will never be the same.

As I relive that experience over and over in my mind, something continues to trouble me about how I responded in the arms of Jesus. Even while being embraced by the Prince of Peace, I couldn't rest and enjoy the moment, and instead felt compelled to do or say something. I really didn't know how to rest. Since that time, this chapter's focus scripture in Hebrews 4 has become a new life goal for my life—to enter the rest that remains for the people of God. In order to enter that rest I must cease from my own labor. Ironically, my own futile efforts have kept me from what I desire most—peace and rest— and I discovered that I had been my own roadblock. I believe He has been beside me all along, waiting for me to realize my limitations and surrender to His will.

Where do we go from here?

Jesus extends an invitation to all of us: "Come unto me, all ye that labor and are heavy laden, and I will give you rest" (Matthew 11:28). Jesus offers to take our labor and our burden and in exchange gives us His rest and peace. But the choice of accepting or rejecting his invitation is ours.

> *The quality of life is not determined by what happens to me but rather by what happens in me as I respond to the situations of life.*

My greatest discovery on the road to recovery from dysfunction has been the power of choice. God created me as a free moral agent with power to choose, but I must understand that every choice I make brings either recompense or reward. The quality of my life is not determined by what happens to me but rather by what happens in me as I respond to the situations of life. Every day I make choices to react to life or to act by establishing a plan of action for my life. Here's my question for you: Are you acting or reacting?

I have found that true freedom and wholeness comes when I am willing to take responsibility for my life and stop blaming others for my condition. While it is okay for me to name my problem, it is never okay for me to blame my problem. I know you will find the same is true for you. As long as the responsibility and focus is on others, it creates a smoke screen behind which we can hide, and an excuse to continue living out a pattern of destructive behavior. There's a new life of freedom and wholeness awaiting each of us on the other side of our next choice. Choices made today determine the level of wholeness we experience tomorrow.

The truth of the matter is that none of our lives are as unique as we believe them to be. All of us have experienced trauma and pain; each of us also carries some level of anger stemming from the circumstances of our life. The more unfairly we feel we have been treated, the greater that level of anger becomes. How we process that anger, therefore, is what determines the quality of our life. Remember, my friend, that anger is simply the response to hidden pain. Anger is not the solution, for only Jesus can heal us and remove the pain we carry.

Processing anger occurs in a variety of ways that are as varied as humanity itself. Daily, it seems, we search for new ways to mask that we have problems with anger. In an attempt to unmask anger, let me share with you just a few of my observations in discovering how anger is mishandled.

1. Alcoholics and sugaraholics soothe their anger.
2. Abusers vent their anger.
3. The depressed rehearse their anger.
4. Workaholics reassign their anger.
5. Gamblers misplace their anger.
6. Pornography addicts ignore their anger.
7. The bitter suppress their anger.
8. Drug addicts escape their anger.
9. Accusers blame their anger.
10. Liars deny their anger.

These are just a few examples of mishandling anger. It's certainly not an exhaustive list, but I'm sure you get the point. Because the quality of my life depends on my choices, my goal is to process anger properly and wisely. Each of us has a choice—continue to mask anger and hide pain, or choose to be honest with God, with ourselves, and with others.

Most people walk around with unresolved anger that negatively affects their life and potential. If a prayerful examination reveals that you are among them, are you willing to admit that your way of handling anger is not working? Are you willing to consider that God's way is best? Are you willing to confront the pain that you have tried so desperately to keep hidden? If you've answered yes to these questions, let me share with you a few things that have helped me during my recovery process. I think they will also serve you well as you start your road to wholeness.

A Safe Place

None of us are willing to share the innermost secrets of our lives with people we are unable to trust. Trust is a real issue in establishing a safe place. My safe place is found in a room full of strangers who don't even know my last name. We meet for group therapy sessions in a neighboring state, two hours from my home. In that setting I can be brutally honest without fear of retaliation and without worry concerning my ministry reputation or what others will think. I can truly be myself while I unload the baggage I've carried since childhood. Begin your search today for a safe place. You'll be glad you did.

An Absolute Commitment to Wholeness

You must become convinced that God does not just desire your healing, He also wants you to be whole. You must take hold of His promises and refuse to surrender to your fleshly desires. Unhealthy patterns are difficult to break, especially those you've diligently practiced throughout your life. But I want to assure you, my friend, that there is hope in God for a better tomorrow.

This is still true: "There hath no temptation taken you but such as is common to man: but God is faithful, who will not suffer you to be tempted above that ye are able; but will with the temptation also make a way to escape, that ye may be able to bear it" (1 Corinthians 10:13). We must hone our ability to recognize God's escape hatches. In every temptation, God provides a way of escape if we remain committed to wholeness.

An Accountability Team

Accountability has become an often spoken, but rarely practiced, catchword. Accountability means giving others the right to question us concerning our attitudes, actions, and progress. But understand that you hold the key to accountability;

you must make yourself accountable before you can expect others to hold you accountable. I used the term "accountability team" on purpose because I have discovered that the best accountability is layered accountability.

Let me explain this layered accountability through an illustration I witnessed several years ago. A speaker had set up a table covered by a beautiful tablecloth at the front of the room. A large glass jar and a number of rocks were on the table. As the speaker talked about how our lives get filled up, he began placing one rock after another into the container until there was no room for more. When he asked the question, "Is this jar full?" everyone responded, "Yes."

But, then he reached beneath the table and pulled out a container filled with gravel. As he continued speaking he poured the gravel around the large rocks until the gravel reached the rim of the jar. Again he paused to ask the same question, "Is this jar full?" The audience did not respond as affirmatively the second time.

He reached under the cloth again and retrieved a container of sand. As he continued his message, he poured sand over the gravel. Through the clear sides of the glass jar we could see the sand filtering through the rock and gravel until it, too, reached the rim.

He paused again to ask, "Is this jar full?" By that point, there was total silence as he reached underneath the cloth for a final container—a pitcher of water. As he poured water into the mixture of sand, gravel and rock, it was easy to see the water as it darkened the contents on its way to the bottom of the jar. He continued pouring until water saturated the materials inside the container and rose to the top. Although the process was slow, eventually he declared, "It's full now!"

As I go through my recovery process, I find the opposite of this illustration is true—I am in the process of emptying the jar. But, the four substances—rock, gravel, sand, and water—used in the speaker's illustration explain the types of relationships that have been essential on my journey to wholeness. We need a healthy balance of truth relationships and love relationships.

I need "rock people," those who help me deal truthfully with the huge issues of my life. With them I can honestly share anything I've experienced and how it has affected me. Those in this category represent my most honest truthful relationships.

Then come the "gravel people" who help me deal with the less dramatic issues that surround, and often result from, the "rocks" in my life. They too are trustworthy friends, with similar problems, who are willing to help. Though their big rock issues may vary slightly, they are still able to relate to my pain and hold me accountable for change. Believe me, though, they are just as vital for wholeness as are the rock people. Often, these people serve as sounding boards for the emotional struggles faced when dealing with big rock issues.

Like sand, "sand people" serve as filters. Relationships with these people play a vital role in helping us sift through new ideas and new concepts for breaking destructive patterns. In my life, the sand people believe in me; they offer the loving encouragement necessary to establish new patterns for a healthier life.

The fourth, and final, level of relationship on a support team should be "water people." During times of struggle, water people bring refreshing. While they may not be in constant relationship throughout the recovery process, they make occasional contact to check on progress and provide cheer along the way. On the journey to recovery, such people are like a breath of fresh air or a drink of cool water.

Illustrating relationships through the examples of rock, gravel, sand, and water helps me understand, evaluate, and properly utilize the relationships God has surrounded me with during my recovery. It is important for each of us to be able to fully evaluate our pain and the struggles we carry. But it is equally important to be able to evaluate and not misuse the relationships that God has given us. Quickly I learned that, in a figurative sense, it is not wise to drop rocks on water people—the result will be big splashes and their calls will stop coming. One's relationship with water people is simply not deep enough to handle such struggles. Nor is it wise to go to a rock or gravel person looking for a soothing or refreshing experience, lest you receive an unwelcome dose of truth in place of a cool drink of water. But all these relationships are vital for us to live a balanced life and to obtain wholeness.

My earnest prayer is that the hints from my journey will give you courage to begin your journey to wholeness. I am firmly convinced that God has not only purchased our wholeness through the sacrifice of His Son, but He has fully provided the relationships necessary for us to experience and enjoy that wholeness. Everything each of us needs is already in place. Why wait? Look around, discover your safe place, pray for at least one rock person to surface in your life right away. Look around for other hurting people you can grow whole with and refuse to live lower than God's ultimate purpose for your life.

As each of us makes our way to the next mountaintop, to the next life-changing encounter with our Lord, I encourage you to enjoy the journey and to not grow weary over the struggles to be faced. Remember that this mountain, like all the mountains before, holds another opportunity to learn another key to mountain living from the Master. Keep climbing! I'll see you on the next mountaintop.

EPILOGUE

Trees are budding, birds chirping. I can even hear the sound of a brook somewhere in the distance as last season's dry leaves crush beneath my feet. It seems as if all nature joins in unison to cheer me on. As the sun peeps through the leaves, I see a clearing ahead. It must be the mountaintop. Demanding the last drop of adrenalin from my sweat-soaked body, I press through a thicket and step over another rock. Grasping a young sapling to steady myself, I pull myself upward, breaking through the bush into the opening. Thank God, I finally made it!

The mountaintop is more beautiful than I ever imagined. Taking a deep breath, I can smell wildflowers that rim a small mountain lake nearby. A breeze cools my face as I pant in an effort to fill my oxygen-starved lungs with thin, mountain air. A huge boulder extends an invitation and I sit.

The view is miles in every direction. Resting from the climb, I begin to evaluate the distance I have already come and how far I have yet to travel. For there, in the distance, is the stark reality of another valley and another mountain. Perhaps it is time, not only to rest, but to reflect on lessons learned during the journey.

I've learned that life has seasons and that wholeness is a journey. I have come to understand that everyone has problems, and that human nature tends to hide them, or even worse, tries to handle them alone. But, I've also discovered that God is always at work in us and around us to bring us to the wholeness He has prepared. God's Word is true—His presence is always with me and He surrounds me with everything and everyone I will ever need to experience wholeness. Along the way I have also come to realize that people are much more forgiving and understanding than I once thought they were.

Where am I now in my journey? I'm over 110 pounds lighter

and much healthier than I once was. The sugar addiction that had me in its clutches has been broken and I have accepted a lifelong challenge to eat right and exercise daily. My mind is more at peace and my relationships are stronger. Unforgiveness, anger, judgmentalism and control have lost their grip, thank God, and now I make my choices with my mind instead of my emotions.

Am I completely whole? Not yet. I'd guess today I'm at about 75 percent of that goal. I still have a mountain or two to climb and a lesson or two to learn. I'm still in a support group and intend to stay there until I'm whole. But I can tell you one thing—I've never been more determined to get there.

To sum it up, I'm still journeying toward wholeness by implementing the lessons Jesus has taught me and that I've shared in this book. I'm completely open to the new lessons awaiting me on the next mountaintop.

Pardon me, but I must go now. Our guide is calling the group together for a short prayer before we descend from the mountaintop to the valley below. Oh yeah, there is one lesson I've learned that I forgot to mention: I've quit traveling alone; it's much too dangerous. By the way, please join our group for prayer. You're welcome to travel with us. The choice is all yours!

ABOUT THE AUTHOR

"NOW IS THE TIME FOR THE CHURCH TO ARISE, TO TAKE ITS PROPER PLACE IN PROVIDING MENTORS AND SPIRITUAL FATHERS TO EQUIP THE NEXT GENERATION TO BE SONS OF GOD AND OPERATE IN THEIR IDENTITY AUTHORITY, AND DESTINY."

Rev. Rick Clendenen

Rick Clendenen believes that one of the greatest needs among today's Christians is for spiritual fathers and mentors. As Jesus did with His disciples, these leaders work closely with a small group of believers, teaching them Kingdom principles and supporting them as they learn, and then sending them to do the same with others.

As Executive Director of World Missions and Evangelism, Inc., it is this vision that has taken Rick to more than 35 countries to speak at pastors' conferences and work with church planters and those who train them. His efforts are helping to establish a network of training and support that is spreading the Gospel of Jesus to millions of people, even among those traditionally the most difficult to reach.

The youngest of fourteen children, Rick was born and raised in a coal mining town in eastern Kentucky. His parents were Christians and his grandfather was a Pentecostal preacher. After becoming a Christian at the age of 17, Rick's commitment to serving others took him through 15 years of volunteer support in a local church. During that time, in response to a burden to help people become functional in the Body of Christ, he taught workshops that helped believers discover their spiritual gifts. That burden continues to motivate him today.

He served as pastor of a church in North Texas for several years, then joined the staff of Christian Fellowship Church in Benton, Kentucky, where he continues to serve the leadership even as he travels extensively. World Missions and Evangelism, Inc., is a worldwide ministry outreach of Christian Fellowship Church that trains missionaries and church planters around the globe.

Rick and his wife, Debbie, have two grown children and one grandson. Their son Richie and daughter-in-law Jenny are the parents of Trey, born in 2004. Their daughter Renee and son-in-law Landon Owen are newlyweds.

Order additional copies of this book, or
contact Rick Clendenen via:
World Missions and Evangelism, Inc.
P. O. Box 790
Benton, KY 42025
Office: (270) 527-8369, Ext. 131